STARTING A SMALL BUSINESS

❈

A GUIDE TO CREATING RELIABLE INCOME AND FINANCIAL INDEPENDENCE IN A CHALLENGING ECONOMY

CAMERON BANKS

STARTING A SMALL BUSINESS

CAMERON BANKS

ISBN: 979-8-9929503-7-3

INTRODUCTION

In today's rapidly shifting economic landscape, the dream of starting a small business resonates with many aspiring entrepreneurs. Yet, the path to creating a reliable income and achieving financial independence is fraught with challenges. The modern economy, characterized by its unpredictability and fierce competition, demands more than just a passion for a particular field or a desire for independence. It requires a strategic approach, careful planning, and a thorough understanding of the multifaceted nature of business operations.

This guide is designed to serve as a comprehensive resource for anyone navigating the complexities of launching and sustaining a small business. From the initial stages of idea generation to the intricacies of market analysis, it offers practical insights and proven strategies tailored to the unique challenges faced by small business owners. Recognizing the importance of aligning personal motivations with market needs, the guide emphasizes introspection and strategic planning as the foundation of entrepreneurial success.

Readers will find detailed explanations on crafting a compelling vision and mission statement, conducting effective market research, and identifying target audiences and their pain points. Furthermore, the guide delves into legal and financial preparation nuances, offering clarity on business structures, tax obligations, and funding options. It also highlights the significance of building a robust business plan that articulates the company's goals and strategies and presents a clear financial roadmap to potential investors.

In addition to strategic planning, the guide underscores the importance of adaptability and resilience. By fostering a culture of learning and innovation, entrepreneurs can swiftly pivot in response to market changes and emerging opportunities. The text also addresses the personal side of entrepreneurship, offering advice on maintaining work-life balance and sustaining motivation over the long haul.

Whether you are a first-time entrepreneur or a seasoned business owner seeking to adapt to new economic realities, this guide will equip you with the knowledge and tools necessary to build a successful and sustainable business. It aims to transform aspirations into tangible achievements through practical advice and real-world examples, paving the way for financial independence and lasting success in a challenging economy.

CONTENTS

INTRODUCTION 1

Laying the Foundation 8

Understanding Your Motivation 8

Generating Business Ideas............................... 10

Evaluating Personal Skills.................................. 13

Aligning with Market Needs............................... 15

Crafting Vision and Mission............................... 17

Conducting Market Research...........................21

Importance of Market Research 21

Identifying Target Segments............................... 23

Competitive Analysis Tools................................. 26

Using Data for Decisions 28

Creating Customer Personas 31

Crafting a Business Plan................................. 34

Structuring for Success....................................... 34

Writing an Executive Summary 36

Detailing Products and Services 38

Developing Marketing Strategies......................... 41

Including Financial Projections 43

Legal and Financial Preparation 46

Choosing Business Structure 46

Navigating Registrations...48

Understanding Tax Obligations 50

Exploring Funding Options 52

Crafting a Financial Plan 55

Building Your Brand 57

Defining Brand Identity 57

Developing Online Presence 59

Leveraging Social Media...61

Content Marketing Strategies 64

Email Marketing Techniques..66

Setting Up Operations...69

Selecting Technology Tools...69

Implementing Project Management 71

Enhancing Team Communication..72

Time Management Strategies..74

Building Lean Business Models..76

Sales and Customer Relations..79

Understanding Sales Process 79

Building Customer Relationships..81

Developing a Pricing Strategy..84

Handling Customer Feedback 86

Creating Loyalty Programs...88

Managing Growth **93**

Identifying Expansion Opportunities 93

Enhancing Product Offerings 95

Utilizing Strategic Partnerships 97

Scaling Operations 99

Adapting to Market Trends 102

Financial Management **105**

Managing Cash Flow 105

Budgeting Effectively 107

Forecasting and Scenarios 109

Working with Financial Advisors 111

Utilizing Accounting Software 113

Networking and Collaborations **116**

Understanding Networking Benefits 116

Crafting an Elevator Pitch 118

Navigating Networking Events 120

Building Online Presence 121

Establishing Partnerships 123

Digital Marketing **126**

Building a Brand Identity 126

Creating a Dynamic Website 128

SEO Basics 130

Leveraging Social Media 132

Analyzing Marketing Metrics 134

Handling Challenges 137

Managing Cash Flow 137

Building Resilience 139

Learning from Mistakes 141

Maintaining Work-Life Balance 142

Dealing with Competition 144

Setting Long-Term Goals 147

Setting Long-Term Goals 147

Celebrating Achievements 149

Staying Connected to Purpose 151

Seeking Inspiration 152

Continuous Learning 155

Ensuring Compliance 158

Understanding Regulations 158

Developing a Compliance Plan 160

Training Staff 162

Monitoring Changes 164

Auditing and Reviews 166

Planning for the Future 169

Developing a Strategic Vision 169

Establishing Succession Plans 171

Building Brand Legacy 173

Ensuring Financial Stability 175

Preparing for Long-Term Success 177

CHAPTER 1

LAYING THE FOUNDATION

Understanding Your Motivation

Starting a small business is not as simple as venturing for financial profit; it requires a lot of cognitive mastery of one's motivations. This fundamental alert the entrepreneurs like a compass for the numerous problems and choices that they will face. The first procedure in this introspective exercise is self-examination of drivers and core motivations. This entails thoroughly examining one's reasons for wanting to begin a business in the first place. It might be triggered by the need to live independently financially, love in a certain sphere, or desire to bring something valuable and important into the world. Understanding these motivations is of great importance as they will be the guiding light that will give clarity and direction in front of obstacles.

Other than the personal drivers, it is necessary to have clear individual goals and aspirations. These goals should be in tandem with their motivations and standards for achievement. Be it achieving a certain level of financial stability, recognition in a given industry, or just a pure hobby or a passion, knowing one's goal simplifies the process of achieving it and keeps one motivated towards pursuing it. The wannabe business stars should align their business ideas to these personal aspirations to create a balanced pursuit of satisfaction in both personal and professional terms.

After one has established clear intentions and aims, then the next step is to develop and polish possible business ideas. This entails brainstorming and appraising ideas to make sure that they correspond with one's motivations and can fulfill needs within the market. In this process, mind mapping and SWOT analysis are a priceless instrument. These techniques enable them to explore different possibilities and evaluate each idea based on its strengths, weaknesses, and opportunities. Such an analytical approach is a way to guarantee that the selected business idea is appealing on a personal level and that it can be successful in the market.

Personal skill and strength appraisal is another very important element in the study of one's motivation. Entrepreneurs will need to assess their capabilities in terms of their skills so that they can embrace ideas that correspond well to their abilities. This self-assessment may point out where one would need to learn more or where one would have to collaborate with others. Different self-assessment tools can help in this process, and they will help individuals develop and align their skills to the needs of the business. This alignment makes the entrepreneur optimally prepared to cope with the needs of their venture of choice.

In addition, the essence of coordinating business concepts with market demands is crucial. A great idea should also be market demand to be successful. By converting the idea into a business, there is a need to conduct a market gap analysis in order to find opportunities whereby the business idea can quench the unmet needs so that it is not just a personal interest but also something that can be marketed. Such an integration of individual drive toward the market demand is critical for long-term business success.

In conclusion, the process of understanding one's motivation is a holistic process that evolves through self-introspection, setting goals, generating ideas, self-evaluation, and market analysis. It is the first and most important step in building a foundation for a successful small business. This focus and market appeal guarantee that the entrepreneur is emotionally involved in his/her pursuit and that he/she is well-placed for success. In this process, potential business owners will be able to create a foundation for their business journey to stand on, giving them the ability to fight through adversity with fortitude and fortitude.

Generating Business Ideas

The birth of a successful small business is a process that often starts with an inspiring idea, but the way to produce such an idea may be complex and numerous. It is the combination of creativity, strategic thinking, and understanding of market requirements. Coming up with business ideas does not mean one has to come up with new things; one must look for opportunities that match what one is passionate about, what one specializes in, and what the market demands.

Introspection is one of the basic methods of generating business ideas. This requires one to go deeper into personal aspirations and longings. If you consider what motivates you, whether it is a passion for technology, a desire to be a part of the community, or the will to transform the industry, you will find something that could be a great source of ideas. This inner re-lifestyle may say something about what sort of business will be effective and personally satisfying.

The other is the analysis of trends in markets and the requirements of consumers. This calls for a keen understanding of the prevailing trends in the market as well as having to predict the trends in the near future. Through the detection of changes in consumer preferences, technology, and the economy, one can determine market gaps through which a new company might come in. This analysis assists in shaping ideas that are not only innovative but also address issues that are relevant and sustainable.

In addition, brainstorming sessions may be very helpful for idea generation. Such sessions are creative and allow thinking outside the box. Mind mapping or brainstorming prompts can stimulate the flow of ideas and generate unexpected and innovative notions. The ability to build a place in which ideas can be openly expressed and discussed without instant evaluation is crucial.

Additionally, the assessment of personal skills and resources is very important. A wonderful business idea usually goes hand in hand with the skill, knowledge, and resources of the entrepreneur. This is a line of harmony, and the chances of the implementation being successful are raised. From a review of what you bring, you can design your business ideas to play within your strengths, thus maximizing your competitive advantage.

Feedback from would-be customers and industry specialists can be priceless. By communicating with such groups using surveys, interviews, or focus groups, it can be learned about what consumers really need and want. This feedback can help sharpen one's ideas to make them innovative and cater to actual market needs. By listening to his or her prospective customers, you will be in a position to gain knowledge on their pain points, thereby being able to offer solutions to your business.

Finally, it is possible to test ideas using small, low-risk experiments such as pilot programs or minimum viable products (MVPs) that can test the viability of the idea without an all-in rollout. This cyclic process enables adjustments from real-world feedback, reduces the risk, and increases the success rate.

Basically, idea generation is an evolving process that involves introspection, market analysis, creativity, and feedback. It calls for an open mind and a predisposition to experiment with different options, keeping to the realities of the market as well as the physical capabilities. Through the application of these principles, wannabe entrepreneurs can come up with novel ideas that will match both their passion and the market.

Evaluating Personal Skills

Knowing one's skills is the first step of the journey of starting a small business. It entails an in-depth reflection on one's strengths, talents, and spots for improvement. This self-assessment is like a compass for prospective entrepreneurs, helping them organize their business objectives while at the same time grounding themselves in their strong suits. The identification of core competencies is the first step in the process; technical skills, interpersonal abilities, and problem-solving abilities are part of core competencies. Identification of these skills is important because they are the skeleton of any successful project.

The first step in this evaluation process is the thorough self-assessment. Several tools and techniques may assist in this introspection, e.g., SWOT analysis, which enables someone to locate his or her strengths, weaknesses, opportunities, and threats. Apart from revealing personal capabilities, this analysis also discovers those areas that need improvements. Also, requesting assessments from peers, mentors, or colleagues could give guidance on one's ability and blind spots.

The personal motivations are also equally important to understand. Entrepreneurs should wonder why they are carrying out a business venture in the first place. Are we driven by the love for a given field, personal desire for financial independence, or the need to solve a certain issue? Many times, such motivations espouse people's values and may affect the direction and nature of the business. Personal skills in synergy with motivations are building the ground for sustainable business.

Further, the evaluation of personal skills should also consider market needs. It is important to make sure that the skills that one has are industry-relevant and can be used to meet market requirements. For example, if the idea of the business is technology-based, then there is a need for excellent technical abilities or an offering to learn good technical skills. Its high chances of success, longevity, and the needs of the market are matched with personal skills.

Another key area of evaluating personal skills is pinpointing the gaps that may stall the progress of business. This means recognizing one's areas of weakness when it comes to what they do and looking for solutions such as further studies, training, or even collaboration with persons with complementary skills. Addressing a partnership may prove to be a strategic move, especially if the partner should present to the business the necessary skills that are not covered by the entrepreneur and that play a critical role in the business.

Moreover, personal skills evaluation is a process rather than a one-time exercise. With the change in business environment, the skills to manage such changes change as well. Entrepreneurs should have continuous learning of skills so as to remain relevant and competitive. This could be in the form of attending workshops on the industry, taking courses, or self-study.

To sum up, the assessment of personal skills is an integral part of the entrepreneurial process. It shows what one can bring to the business and areas where one needs to improve. When entrepreneurs make use of personal skills to meet their business objectives and market needs, they can develop a solid foundation for their ventures. This self-consciousness and desire for growth not only increase the odds of business success but are also helpful in making one a fulfilled person.

Aligning with Market Needs

In this fast-moving world of small business, it is vital to understand and follow the needs of the market in order to succeed. This process starts with thorough market research, which is the foundation for any effective business strategy. When going through the market, entrepreneurs can uncover gaps and openings that the business can specifically fill. This entails the collection of data on existing market trends, consumer behavior, and the level of competition.

Once entrepreneurs conduct research, they are able to identify specific needs in the target market. This step is very important because not only will it bring out potential opportunities, but it also will help them develop products or services that consumers will really need. Entrepreneurs should consider solving unfulfilled needs or those segments that are not properly represented in the market. This understanding enables them to customize their offerings so as to bridge these gaps, making it more likely for them to succeed.

Once market needs have been identified, a business model in tune with these findings must be developed. This entails creating products or services that target the identified needs. A successful alignment with the needs of the market presupposes an in-depth knowledge of the target audience, its preferences, purchasing behavior, and the pain points. Feeling for the consumer, businesses are able to develop solutions that meet not just the expectations of the market but also the expectations of the market.

Furthermore, it is important to be in touch with market changes. Markets are not static; they adapt according to different factors like technological advancements, economic changes, and changes in customer preferences. Entrepreneurs should remain vigilant and flexible, closely watching these changes and developing their strategies accordingly. This could be a shift in the business model, outlining new offerings and even new markets.

Feedback loops are another important element of conforming to the needs of the market. Through solicitation and use of feedback established by customers, businesses have a chance to improve their range of products and services to suit consumers' needs. This constant conversation with the customers makes it possible for business organizations to remain in tune with the customers' needs, building loyalty and trust. Additionally, using data analytics can give important business insights into the customer's behavior and how they prefer to operate, and thus, better choices are made in a business.

In addition, communication of value is key. After a business has come up with offerings that match the market requirements, it must express these offerings' distinct value to the consumer. This will entail the creation of an exciting value proposition that will focus on the benefits and differentiators of the product or service. A well-formulated value proposition not only attracts potential customers but also gives the business an edge over its competitors.

Lastly, businesses should look out for strategic partnerships that can be used to strengthen their capacity to address market needs. Cooperation with other companies may grant access to new technologies, distribution channels, or customers, multiplying the reach and the impact of the company. Such partnerships should be carefully chosen in order to have their goals and values aligned, which would combine efforts to form a coherent strategy for market alignment.

In conclusion, it is a constant evolvement process that requires absolute perceptiveness, malleability, and inner knowledge of the envisaged market. With market research, interactive communication with target customers, and strategic collaboration, entrepreneurs can design a sound business strategy that could help them serve and even predict their market needs in the long term, as well as ensure sustainability in the business.

Crafting Vision and Mission

A clear vision and mission in the course of developing a small business are some of the pillars that underpin the enterprise toward fulfilling its objectives. The vision statement is the culmination of the long-term goals of the business, revealing what success will appear like in the future. It serves as a beacon that guides and inspires the founders as well as the working team and other stakeholders involved.

It takes introspection and foresight to write a vision statement. It entails visualization of the ultimate impact that the business wants to offer to its customers, industry, and the community. The statement should be achievable yet challenging, seeming to be what the business wants to be. A clearly laid out vision statement not only inspires but also harmonizes everyone's efforts to a common direction, translating to actions directed towards a common end goal.

Mission statement development is also very important as it is the working center of the business. Although the vision statement caters to the "what" of the business's future, the mission statement deals with the "why" and "how" of its everyday operations. It briefly defines what the business ventures into and the underlying values and principles that govern its business as well as decision-making.

A strong mission statement should resonate with an internal and external entity. To the employees, it brings certainty and direction, which instills a sense of belonging and reason for being in the organization. For the customers and stakeholders, it gives a glimpse of what the business is prioritizing and what it is committed to, earning trust and credibility.

In order to be coherent and effective, the vision and the mission statements should match closely. This correlation promotes the fact that the long-term objective of the business is reflected in its short-term actions and strategies. It makes a comprehensive account that stakeholders may understand and favor, with them having a collective voice in working towards the goals of the business.

The creation of these statements involves not only the leadership team but also includes contributions from stakeholders. Including the employees in the process can make the buy-in better, and the statements will represent employees' diverse perspectives. This form of collective perspective also reveals the exclusive secrets that enhance the contents, thus making them more reflective of the culture and ambitions of the business.

Its formulation, followed by its effective communication with all the stakeholders, is very important once it is made. This communication can be of different kinds, ranging from internal meetings and workshops to external marketing and presentation. Substantial messaging throughout all the platforms guarantees that the vision and the mission are embraced and comprehended by all people involved in the business, either as the owner or those who are working for the business, indirectly or directly.

In summary, the creation of a vision and mission is not a one-time activity but a continuous exercise. As the business situation changes over time, these observations might be reviewed to confirm that they reflect the growth and the changing nature of the business. Suppose a small business holds on to a simple yet powerful vision and mission. In that case, navigating through the complexities of the marketplace will be attainable, thus setting the foundation for the long-term success of the business.

CHAPTER 2

CONDUCTING MARKET RESEARCH

Importance of Market Research

Market research is a crucial basis for a starting entrepreneur who aspires to start a successful small business. It offers a systematic guideline for understanding how the market environment operates, which is important when making business decisions. By going into market research with full diligence, entrepreneurs are likely to discover incalculable insights that can dramatically impact the path that their business may take.

The identification and analysis of the target market are critical parts of market research. This requires a deep investigation of the demographics, likes and dislikes, and the habits of potential customers. The segmentation of the market helps enterprises adjust their products or services to suit the actual requirements of various groups of customers, which increases the possibility of success. Knowing who their customers are, what they want, and how they behave allows businesses to position themselves toward the market strategically.

In addition, market research helps identify market trends and consumer patterns. Knowing what is happening in this area, businesses can prepare for the changes and keep up to date with the latest trends in the market. This move is vital at a time of a rapidly changing business environment where consumer tastes may change rapidly. Through market research, businesses can innovate and modify their offerings to meet the needs at present and in the future.

The other key element in market research is competitor analysis. It means evaluating the strengths and weaknesses of competitors already in the market so that the businesses may find what they are lacking to fill in the gaps. If businesses can get to understand the competitive landscape, they can come up with unique selling propositions that will distinguish them from their competitors. This differentiation is important for customers to draw in what is a highly competitive market.

The market research is also a basis for risk management. Through the observation of possible challenges and threats in the market, businesses are able to develop ways to prevent these risks. It is immeasurably worth it, as it prepares businesses for unknown situations that, if left unchecked, might bring businesses to a halt. Also, market research can show companies how they can extend and grow, meaning that they can take advantage of new trends and untapped markets.

In addition, data-driven decision is an important result of successful market research. Companies can use gathered and analyzed data to base their decisions on knowledge aided by empirical evidence rather than conjecture. This lowers the chances of expensive mistakes and enhances the chances of bringing the desired business outcomes. Data analytics tools and techniques can be used to pull information from the overwhelming amounts of data obtained through market research in order to strengthen decision-making processes.

Finally, the approach to market research creates a customer-centric nature, which is critical in establishing great relationships with customers. Through knowledge of what customers need and prefer, business enterprises can streamline their products, services, and marketing strategies to benefit their customers. This emphasis on customer satisfaction not only provides customer loyalty but also improves the total brand reputation.

In other words, market research is not just a portion of preliminary activities to business planning; it is a continuous effort that brings continuous growth and success to the business. Continuous market research enables companies to be agile, competitive, and responsive to the unending market dynamics, thereby ensuring their long-term viability and prosperity.

Identifying Target Segments

A good business strategy starts with facts about the target market segments. Discovery of these segments requires an in-depth analysis of possible customer groups, needs, behaviors, and preferences. This process is important because, through this process, businesses can adjust their products and services to suit the individual demands of a given segment in order to enhance market fit and greater customer satisfaction.

First of all, get down to demographic and psychographic analysis. Demographics are the quantitative description of the market in terms of age, gender, income, education, and occupation. This information is used to develop a profile of potential customers so that they can know who their potential customers might be. Psychographic analysis, in turn, seeks out qualitative properties like lifestyle, values, interests, and opinions. This deeper understanding helps to create marketing messages that will strike on personal levels and appeal to the emotions and personal values of the customer.

When the demographic and psychographic profile is done, businesses could then divide the market into distinct groups. Measurable, accessible, substantial, differentiable, and actionable – these are both the criteria of each segment. Measurable segments help the business quantify the size of its purchasing ability, and accessibility enables these target groups to be accessible through marketing channels. Substantial segments are large enough to be profitable; differentiable segments show different needs that justify tailored marketing. Lastly, the actionable segments are those for which the company can create effective programs.

Other than demographic and psychographic considerations, more emphasis is being placed on behavior-based segmentation. This entails reviewing consumer behavior, such as purchase, brand interaction, and use of the product. By understanding these behaviors, businesses will be able to forecast future purchasing patterns and act according to these foundations. For example, regular buyers could be subjected to loyalty programs while occasional buyers would be offered promotional deals.

Once segments are defined, businesses need to prioritize them, depending on their strategic goals and resources. Not all segments are equal in terms of their value, and the resources needed to penetrate them effectively may vary. Evaluation of the potential profitability of each segment, with respect to the company's long-term objectives, is critical. This prioritization means that marketing will focus on the most promising opportunities at the highest return on investment.

Another of the key elements of target segment identification is competitor analysis. By knowing the competitor's strengths and weaknesses to serve different segments, opportunities for differentiation can be unearthed. In order to differentiate themselves in the market, businesses can opt to provide better value than the competition or fill in the gaps in a segment. Such strategic positioning might be a great differentiator in highly competitive markets.

Lastly, creating unique value propositions specific to each segment is critical. This proposition must outline the benefits and value proposition that the business brings for every particular group. By linking the value proposition to the demand and the desire of each segment, businesses make strong arguments for customers to consider their products or services against rival alternatives.

In essence, target segment identification is not just a way of breaking the market into fragments. It's about knowing who the customers are, what they prize, and how best to reach and serve them. This strategic move will make it easy for businesses to address the varied needs of their market, creating better customer relationships and sustainable growth.

Competitive Analysis Tools

Understanding the competitive environment is essential in the context of modern business. Entrepreneurs and business owners need to obtain the right tools to analyze their competitors and create a space in the market. In-depth competitive analysis helps businesses to understand their strengths, weaknesses, and opportunities. Refers to threats – SWOT Analysis gives the backbone to what is strategic planning.

The competitor matrix is one of the basic tools in a competitive analysis. This matrix enables companies to compare their products and services systematically with those of their competition. By comparing competitors and comparing a range of attributes, including prices, features, customer service, and market share, a business can point out what it does well and where it falls behind. Such a rigorous format facilitates the identification of unique selling propositions and strategies to improve competitive advantages.

Another central tool that gives a holistic impression of a business's internal and external environment is a SWOT analysis.

Assessing strengths and weaknesses allows businesses to focus on core competencies and improve on their weakness. Opportunities and threats analysis, however, is useful in identifying possible market gaps and external threats that may affect the operations of the business. This dual analysis prepares businesses in a way that they are well prepared to take advantage of opportunities while defraying risks.

Data analytics has developed into an inseparable tool in competitive analysis. Nowadays, businesses have access to a great mass of information thanks to the coming of big data, which can be used to support strategic decision-making. Such tools as Google Analytics, insights from social media, customer relationship management (CRM) systems, etc., give valuable information on customer behavior, preferences, and trends. This information, when examined, can shed light on the market dynamics and requirements of the customers and help businesses fine-tune their offerings to suit the customers better.

In addition, benchmarking is a critical tool that entails a comparison of a business process and performance metrics with industry bests/best practices of other firms. This process enables businesses to identify those areas in which they can improve their efficiency, lower their costs, and improve their quality. If the performance standards are established following industry leaders, businesses can work towards perpetual improvement and innovation.

Other than these tools, scenario planning is one of the strategic tools that will assist businesses in planning for future challenges and opportunities. If business prognosticates possible scenarios and their potential effects, firms can formulate supply strategies in line with the shifts in the market settings. This preventive measure means changes in the competitive environment will not blindside businesses.

Companies can also use market research tools to obtain qualitative and quantitative information about competitors. Surveys, focus groups, and interviews give rich consumer insight into perceptions and preferences, whereas market reports and industry analyses will give a broader view of market trends and competitor strategies. These observations are priceless to businesses that would like to tune their competitiveness levels and tailor their items to suit the demands of the market.

Finally, the ability of the competitive analysis tools to deliver actionable insights is what can make them effective. The analysis methodologies of businesses need to be refined, and businesses need to keep pace with new tools and technologies that could improve their competitive intelligence. In that way, they are able to stay ahead of the competition and achieve long-term success in a fast-changing market environment.

Using Data for Decisions

Making the right informed decisions that would propel a business in a fast-moving small business environment may heavily rely on how maximally one can utilize data. Data-driven decision-making implies systematic collection, analysis, and interpretation of data to inform strategic business management. Such an approach not only ensures better decisions are made but also ensures that the results remain competitively advantageous in unraveling market dynamics and consumer behavior.

Data collection is the first step in deploying data for the good of making decisions. This can be done in different ways, such as surveys, customer feedback, web analysis, and social media analysis. These data sources are important sources of information relating to customer preferences, purchasing behaviors, and emerging market trends. Through a collection of data from these varied sources, businesses can create a whole picture of the market landscape.

As soon as data collection has been done, data analysis becomes the next important step. This entails data processing from raw data to useful insights. Companies may use different forms of data analysis tools, like statistical analysis, trend analysis, and predictive modeling, to interpret data. Such tools help to discern patterns and correlations that may not come to the eye right away, meaning businesses can forecast market movements and consumer demands with ease.

The implementation of insights into decision-making should follow it. This integrates the insights drawn from data into strategic and operational decisions. For example, data can guide product development by showing consumer preferences, and hence, businesses will be in a position to make products that fit particular customer needs. Equally, data can inform marketing strategies in determining the best channels and messages to use in order to reach their target audience.

What is more, data-driven decision-making creates an accountability culture and an ever-improving environment around an organization. Companies can then track progress and evaluate adjustments to the strategies based on the metrics and key performance indicators (KPIs) set from this data. This cyclic process of testing, measuring, and refining strategies will allow us to align the business decisions with the realities of markets and organization goals.

In addition to internal decision-making, data is also integral to external communication with users. Effective and inspiring data visualizations can strengthen credibility and trust with investors, business partners, and customers. Visualization of data using charts, graphs, and dashboards makes any complex information easier to present and more convincing, allowing for convenient communication and collaboration.

Yet data integrity and privacy must be maintained during the decision-making process. There is a need to expect businesses to abide by ethical codes and regulatory controls on data collection and application. This requires strict measures in data protection to protect sensitive information for the purpose of retaining consumer confidence.

To conclude, data for decisions is not simply about access to information but about how to use this information to parse it into actionable insights. Through data-driven practices deep-rooted into business practices, small businesses can improve aggressiveness, streamline operations, and accelerate sustainable growth. This strategic application of data leaves businesses capable of making informed decisions that will respond not only to present but also to future market calls.

Creating Customer Personas

Being aware of the desires and priorities of potential customers is very important for any small enterprise that needs to be successful in the competitive environment. The art of defining detailed customer personas is an adventure into the lives, behaviors, and desires of your target market, establishing a definite map that defines your marketing and product development strategy.

Start by collecting extensive data concerning your potential customers. This includes demographic data, which includes age, gender, income level, and education, and the psychographic component, which digs into their values, interests, and lifestyle choices. This information can be gathered in different ways, which include surveys, interviews, and social media analysis, and it can be used to determine what motivates and challenges your audience.

Segmenting your audience to come up with distinct groups who share certain characteristics is the next step after completing the data collection process. Such segmentation will enable the development of unique personas, each corresponding to a different part of your market. A persona may be a young professional who appreciates convenience and technology or a middle-aged parent only interested in family-friendly products and services.

Every persona should be well-defined, giving a clear picture of the individual. Add a name, occupation, and a back story explaining their daily life and how they make decisions. This narrative makes the data more human, thus supporting the ability to empathize with the customer's needs. Spotlight their objectives, their problem, the kind of solution they desire, and their method of communicating and media PC.

The addition of actual quotes and anecdotes from customer interactions can fill these personas with depth and determine the nuances of people's viewpoints. This human aspect is critical to ensuring that the marketing strategies speak to the targeted audience and that the connections are not only relevant but real.

Customer personas are not static; they need to change from new insights and trends. Keep updating these profiles as you keep on receiving more data through continuous interactions and feedback. This iterative process helps keep your understanding of the customer relevant and accurate so that you can better target customers.

In addition, customer personas are a useful tool to integrate your team into your goals. By applying a collective identity to who the customer is, personas help align the marketing, sales, and product development teams toward the same objectives and plan of action. This is a way of bringing the business operations into a more cohesive and focused manner to improve consequent customer experience.

Lastly, the development of customer personas is not merely about identifying those customers who buy from you but about figuring out what those customers need in the future and what they might evolve into. This vision helps your business to stay dynamic and flexible in a dynamic market, requiring that your products and services remain relevant to the constantly changing demands of your audience.

Essentially, the development of customer personas is a core activity of strategic planning that provides a lens through which to see and service your customers better. By allocating the time and capital to this process, small businesses can tailor their marketing strategies to a deeper level of personalization, which consequently would increase customer satisfaction, yielding business success.

CHAPTER 3

CRAFTING A BUSINESS PLAN

Structuring for Success

A well-structured business is much like a well-oiled machine, where all the parts work together to make the company run smoothly as a team. In the realm of small business, structuring is important for making things run smoothly day-to-day and also helps set up a strong base that can handle growth and changes over time. This process starts by knowing the different types of business structures and what each one is best for. Whether you pick a sole proprietorship, a partnership, an LLC, or a corporation, the type of business structure you choose will affect things like what taxes you have to pay and how much personal risk you take if something goes wrong.

A sole proprietorship, for instance, is the easiest way to start a business and gives you the most control, which makes it good for people who want to go it alone. However, it also means the owner is personally responsible, which means they could lose some of their things if something goes wrong. Partnerships, on the other hand, mean people have to share what they do and what they have, but they need to make sure they agree on the rules so any problems that come up don't get out of hand. LLCs are in between a standard partnership and a corporation, so they give some protection for owners but still make it easy for the business to move and change as needed, which is why lots of small businesses choose them. Corporations, though a bit harder to set up, give the strongest protection from personal legal issues and are better for people who want to grow a lot or bring in investors.

The decision-making process should include carefully looking at how each structure affects things, like who controls the business, who's responsible if something goes wrong, taxes we might have to pay, and if the business can grow easily in the future. It's essential to think about how much you want to say in things, what kind of risks you're okay with taking, and if your business might need more money sometimes. Real-world examples can show you how other businesses in a similar field handled these choices, making it easier for new business owners to understand what to do.

After choosing the business structure, you should pay attention to legal requirements and registration. Different industries and locations require you to get different permits and licenses. Understanding local laws and making sure businesses stay in compliance are key to avoiding expensive penalties. Being registered correctly allows the business to be trusted and admired by its customers and partners.

At the same time, it is vital to put a strong financial system in place. It is also important to set up your business bank account, get your accounting practices arranged, and have ways to manage your records. Correct financial reports help with taxes and also tell you how your business is doing financially, helping you make the right decisions. Experts in finance, such as accountants, can help you design a suitable financial layout for both efficiency and compliance.

It is also essential to keep in mind the needs of the people working in the company. Even a small team should have clear roles assigned to everyone so every member is able to support the business goals. When roles are clear and team members understand each other, there is less chance for confusion, and more work gets done.

Above all, it is very important to be flexible in life. A business structure designed to be flexible and agile tends to have a greater chance of succeeding in today's market. Checking the structure and how the company works on a regular basis helps it meet its objectives and adapt when needed. Therefore, to achieve success, a business must be carefully planned, and its leaders must be ready to make informed choices along the way.

Writing an Executive Summary

But, the executive summary is the main part of a business plan that clearly presents and persuades readers about the plan. Since investors or key stakeholders may only read the executive summary, it should be built with accuracy and care. Attention should be caught immediately, and an interesting outline should be given that prompts the reader to read the rest of the business plan.

The beginning of the story needs to captivate the audience. First sentences should impress upon the reader why your business matters and create interest in your message. It is not limited to expressing information but rather includes a narrative that brings the opportunity to life visually. You should show what makes the business different from others and also support the reason it could do well in the market.

The main highlights of the business plan need to be quickly and clearly explained. This part should cover the core ideas of the business, the current market situation, how the growth opportunity will be seized, and the forecasts that prove the business can be profitable. The key is to simplify complicated information so that the explanation is easy to follow and still holds a reader's attention.

It is important for the style and feel of the executive summary to match the brand identity and the demographic it wants to communicate with. Regardless of the kind of writing, the tone should be clear and not include technical words so that everyone can understand it. The voice that a brand finds should suit its message and mission.

Incorporating key financial highlights is another critical component. These figures should be presented in a way that is easy to understand, focusing on the most compelling financial metrics that demonstrate the business's potential for growth and return on investment. These might include revenue projections, profit margins, and break-even analyses.

Financial key points should not be forgotten. The figures should be organized so that anyone can analyze them, including the numbers that highlight the business's possible growth and returns. Some of the things these might contain are estimated income, margins, and break-even information.

In addition, the executive summary should also highlight the members of the team involved in the business. Talking about the skills and backgrounds of the main team members can prove to potential investors that the team is capable of carrying out the business plan.

A key rule for an executive summary is to make it brief. It needs to be short and focused, yet informative, so that the reader gets a good idea of the business's prospects. You must make sure that every small detail helps the reader understand the message of the text.

In the end, the executive summary should show the reader why the business is worth supporting and what it could accomplish. It also involves showing the reader how the business can benefit them and what the chance is for them. It requires crafting smart messages, telling appealing stories, and effectively bringing out what makes the business different. As a result, the executive summary encourages investors and stakeholders to back the company.

Detailing Products and Services

The detailed listing of products and services mainly guides the way you describe what your business does. We will look at the main purpose of this part, which is a key element in any business plan that aims to explain the main services. To start, describe the items or services in detail, making it clear what makes them stand out. It includes a clear story that links the solutions or reasons the products are designed to satisfy the needs of the target market. Instead of only listing the features, the copy focuses on the benefits to attract customers' interest and solve their problems.

One important thing to do when detailing is to explain what makes the company's offerings stand out from others. You have to talk about the distinctive elements of your products compared to others. No matter which one of these stands out, it needs to be made clear so that customers will recognize the value. Separating the business in this manner attracts buyers and builds a brand that is strong enough to survive in the market.

How the project is built is another important thing to cover. It describes the journey of the product or service from its start all the way to when it was launched. Describing the process makes the offer more valuable in the eyes of consumers. This process often involves prototyping, testing, and updating, proving a dedication to good craftsmanship and creativity. With transparent sharing, businesses can build a sense of trust with potential clients and stakeholders, as it shows an orderly and purposeful product development way.

It is important to add future product or service plans to the strategy in addition to what is currently on offer. It demonstrates that the company is well prepared for the future and can adapt, putting stakeholders at ease. With an effective product roadmap, a clear path forward for the product can be seen, along with plans for new features and growth that line up with market needs and what customers want.

It is critical to include what customers say during the development process. Using surveys, focus groups, and face-to-face interactions can provide valuable ideas to improve the service further. In this process, the company Refines its products and encourages customers to stay loyal to them.

Developing products and services now relies heavily on technology. Making use of technology can cause businesses to come up with offerings that are personalized, efficient, and effective. That could mean using AI to provide custom services or including IoT technology to make products more useful. Not only do these new technologies improve what customers get, but they also help the business lead in its sector.

Sustainability and focusing on social responsibility in developing products can greatly improve how the public views a brand. More and more, people care about companies that choose environmentally friendly resources, environmentally friendly ways of making goods, and ethical working environments. By doing these things, businesses attract more eco-friendly customers and make a positive impact worldwide.

All in all, describing your products and services goes beyond creating a list of them. It means building a story that shares your company's value, innovative ideas, and vision. It helps bring in and keep customers while also supporting the company's long-term goals.

Developing Marketing Strategies

In the realm of small business development, making a solid marketing plan is really important if you want your business to keep growing and do well in the long run. The journey starts by really getting to know who your customers are, like dividing them into groups and figuring out where your brand fits in the market. Segmentation means breaking apart the market into different groups by looking at things like age, interests, and how people act. This lets the business adjust what it offers to fit exactly what each group of customers wants, which helps them feel happier with the company and more likely to keep coming back.

Once the market is split into different groups, the next thing to do is to find the best place for your business to fit in each group. This means coming up with a simple and straight-to-the-point description that explains why your business stands out and what it offers people. The positioning statement should show what makes the business different from others and what benefits customers will get if they pick its products or services. This isn't only about not being the same as everyone else; it's about being clearly better at things that are important to the people your product or service is meant for.

With a good grasp of the market and knowing where the brand should fit, the next step is to decide which marketing methods and platforms to use. In today's digital age, having a good marketing plan usually means using a mix of both online and offline marketing methods. Digital marketing strategies might include things like using social media, making your website show up in searches, sending out emails, and creating helpful content. Each of these channels has its strengths, and by using them, organizations can better connect with different groups of people interested in their product or service. Traditional marketing tools like print ads, mailers, and events are still really important, especially if you want to connect with people in your community or groups who might not use the internet as much.

An important part of planning marketing strategies is establishing realistic goals and measurements for sales. Goals need to match the major goals of the company and should be SMART, which means they should be Specific, Measurable, Achievable, Relevant, and Time-bound. Having well-defined KPIs makes it possible to review the success of your marketing and plan better strategies for the future.

Identifying the right price for your product or service is an important aspect of a winning marketing plan. Factors that should be considered when figuring out the correct pricing model include production expenses, competitors' rates, how much customers think the product is worth, and what customers are used to paying. Whichever strategy is used, cost-based, value-based, or based on competition, it must match the business's objectives and how it is perceived in the market.

In addition, the strategy needs to address the planning of financial forecasts. Knowledgeable Finance Managers also ensure that comprehensive financial statements of income and cash flow are created with realistic data and assumptions. They also help estimate if the marketing strategies are profitable and secure money from those who provide funds.

Lastly, a good marketing strategy has to be flexible. Businesses ought to change their strategies when consumer habits, competitors' actions, and new technologies change in the market. Watching market trends and data on a regular basis allows a business to know when it is necessary to change its marketing strategy to stay on top.

Including Financial Projections

Projecting your expected finances is an important part of setting up a new small business. These projections play a vital role in both planning and when asking for money from outside sources. They let entrepreneurs understand the possible financial situation the company might face by projecting future incomes, expenses, and profits.

It is necessary, at the outset, to build thorough financial statements. These consist of income statements, balance sheets, and cash flow statements. Every statement fulfills its unique reason for being there. Profitability for a specific period comes from the income statement, the balance sheet shows the business's current financial condition, and the cash flow statement monitors all cash transactions in and out of the business. When put together, these records become the base of financial projections.

For financial projections to be accurate, they depend on using practical assumptions and dependable figures. Available historical data should be studied to look for trends that help you make predictions for the future. If there are no historical records, using trends in the market and industry markers becomes useful. It is necessary to be somewhat cautious in your assumptions to take into account risks and possible changes in the market.

Conducting a break-even analysis is a key part of sound financial planning. It allows us to figure out when the business can pay for its expenses and make a profit. Setting the right sales goals and deciding on prices is easier once you know your break-even point.

Additionally, the creation of scenarios allows managers to be ready for many different possible results. If business owners work out the best, worst, and most likely scenarios, they can be ready for future problems and have plans to respond. It helps strengthen our ability to cope and also guides us in choosing when we are unsure what to do.

You should always go through and update your financial forecasts as things in the market and business performance change. Setting reviews into a calendar allows business owners to look at their progress and make the required changes. To keep track of the business's money and make informed decisions, it is important to set KPIs, such as growth in revenue and the cost of acquiring new customers.

Furthermore, financial projections play an important role in presenting to investors. Investors are focused on checking whether a business is likely to succeed financially and how much they could earn if they invest. Financial projections that are well constructed can give confidence to new investors.

Financial projections are just as much a matter of strategic thinking as they are about counting and budgeting. Having a positive attitude and being realistic, creative, and analytical is necessary in management. Building precise and changing financial forecasts strengthens the financial base of any business.

CHAPTER 4

LEGAL AND FINANCIAL PREPARATION

Choosing Business Structure

Selecting the right kind of business structure is an important choice that can really shape how things go for a new business. This choice not only changes how a business pays taxes but also changes how owners are personally responsible for the company's debts, how easily the business can get money from investors, and how much freedom it has to grow in the future. Entrepreneurs need to think carefully about these things before they choose a business setup that fits well with what they want to achieve and the things going on in their own lives.

In the realm of business structures, the sole proprietorship is usually seen as the easiest and most popular choice, often picked by people starting their small businesses. This structure gives the owner full control over the business, but it also means that anything the owner owns can be used to pay off business debt or lawsuits since, in the eyes of the law, the business and the owner are the same. This can be good for people who want to be their boss and keep things simple, but the fact that you might have to pay for their treatments out of your pocket can be a big downside.

Partnerships, one of the more common types, let two or more people split the profits and work together on what needs to be done in the business. This structure can really help when people or companies work together to share resources and ideas. Still, it's important to have a strong agreement to handle any problems or possible arguments that might come up. Partners are usually both responsible together and separately for paying back business debts, which can make it harder to manage their finances.

For people looking for some protection from liability while still having the freedom to manage their business as they see fit, limited liability companies (LLCs) are a good choice. An LLC gives its owners, called members, a similar level of protection from business risks as a corporation does, and the owners also get to enjoy the tax benefits that a partnership gets. This structure is popular for how easily the business can share money and decisions among owners, but it can be harder to set up than starting up as a sole proprietor or a partnership.

S and C corporations are structured to protect an owner's assets from problems in the business. A C Corporation is required to pay taxes on its own, which may result in receiving double taxes on dividends paid out to shareholders, but it allows companies to raise unlimited funds by selling their shares. In contrast, the profits in an S Corporation are passed to the owners' tax forms so they are not taxed twice, although there are limits on how many shareholders an S Corporation can have.

When selecting a legal structure, it is important to consider not just the current state of the business but its future needs, too. Investment needs, the wish for control, and aims for the future should all play a role when making the decision. In planning for fast growth, a business could use a corporate structure to easily raise money by issuing shares.

The decision on what type of business to form is an important one, not to be taken lightly. You should be able to understand how each answer fits with personal and business aspirations. It is recommended that entrepreneurs seek advice from legal and financial experts to confirm that their choice of structure matches their business aims and keeps their wealth safe. This decision lays the groundwork for all the business's future activities and plans.

Navigating Registrations

Registering your small business is one of the most important steps that needs close attention. It makes sure a business can operate within the law and with all proper regulations. To start, you should pick a business name that is unique and available for use. The company's name should reflect its brand and aims and make it easy to distinguish itself from others.

The following stage is registering the chosen name with the correct authority within the government. The process changes from one location to another and depends on how the business is organized, so entrepreneurs must know the rules for their place. In some cases, sole proprietors have to get a Doing Business As (DBA) registration, but corporations and LLCs must follow official steps to incorporate.

Obtaining an Employer Identification Number (EIN) from the Internal Revenue Service (IRS) is an important step as well. You need this number for your business's taxes and to handle necessary paperwork, such as opening a bank account, hiring workers, and filling in tax returns. Completing the EIN application is usually quick and can often be done via the Internet, allowing for fast entry into running a business officially.

After taking care of the foundational steps, it is important to know about the licenses and permits needed for the company's operations. Requirements may be quite different depending on the industry, business area, and what the company does. Health and safety permits are a must for restaurants, compared to the specialist contractor licenses that are needed by businesses involved in construction. Reaching out to local chambers of commerce or industry associations can give you helpful information about these requirements.

You will need to prepare detailed applications, often including proof of insurance, go through the zoning approval process, and pass some personal background checks to secure the required permits and licenses. It is important to check all your work carefully at this point because missing or inaccurate parts can cause delays.

Complying with the law involves more work than just registering. Firms should always make sure their permits and licenses are renewed on time and be ready for changes in the regulations that could affect them. Always remembering when paperwork is due and keeping accurate records can stop any lapse that could result in fines or the business closing down.

Going through the registration process is essential for setting up any business that is both reputable and legally legitimate. Though it means putting in time and money, the reward is a business that can expand and succeed. Doing these things properly allows entrepreneurs to create a firm and adaptable business that stands up well to competitors.

While it can be complicated, it helps business owners learn more about their business environment and the laws that apply to companies like theirs. As a result, it serves as an important part of the strategy for running a successful small business.

Understanding Tax Obligations

Anyone looking to start a small business needs to understand how taxes impact your business's financial state and daily operations. It is important to understand the different taxes your business can have, such as federal, state, and local taxes. Because the rules, deadlines, and filing needs are different for every level, you must stay on top of things and be organized.

Businesses at the federal level are required by the Internal Revenue Service (IRS) to comply with income tax rules. For each business type, be it a sole proprietorship, partnership, corporation, or LLC, specific tax forms and procedures must be used. For a sole proprietor, income from the business is declared on their personal tax form. However, corporations will be taxed on their business income separately. Knowing about these differences matters a lot in preventing penalties and being compliant.

Some states will add income taxes, and others collect sales tax on what they sell so state taxes can be quite different. Business owners should take time to understand all the tax requirements in their state to avoid breaking the law. In addition, business entities may have to pay property taxes on their company buildings and may also owe municipal business taxes, which can make things more complicated.

Apart from the basic taxes, companies also have to pay self-employment taxes related to contributions to Social Security and Medicare. Sole proprietors and partners in a partnership are responsible for dealing with all parts of these taxes, which is why this matters to them. Sometimes, you may be required to pay estimated taxes during the year, helping to prevent penalties for not paying enough in taxes.

Various deductions and credits can be used to reduce the taxes that small business owners must pay. Typically, people claim deductions for setting up a home office, paying business travel costs, and paying for employee benefits, all of which bring down the amount of taxable income. Benefits such as extra credits for energy conservation or targeted group hiring can save you lots of tax.

It is important to keep detailed and accurate records, both for your taxes and to look for possible deductions. If your company follows a strong bookkeeping system, you can easily find all receipts and payments needed during the tax season.

Having a tax expert guide can be truly valuable for those new to business and tax rules. An experienced accountant can guide you through taxation issues, improve your tax planning, and ensure you do not miss deadlines.

All in all, handling and meeting tax duties takes continual effort, and it requires being prepared ahead of time. Staying aware of tax rules and consulting experts when needed allows small business owners to take care of their taxes, ensuring their business stays financially healthy and can grow.

Exploring Funding Options

Having the necessary financial support is vital when starting a new business to help it succeed in the long run. There are many ways to find funding, and each one has particular strengths and weaknesses. Most people like bank loans and lines of credit because they expect a regular repayment schedule and low interest rates. Yet, many banks ask for a strong credit track record and a large amount of collateral, making it hard for new entrepreneurs to borrow money.

For companies that seek out other ways to fund their businesses, angel investors and venture capitalists may be good options. They are able to provide money needed by the company in return for a share of the business. This comes with a portion of your business's ownership, but it also gives you access to wise investment advice and chances to meet and work with others in the industry. Nevertheless, sharing decision-making duties may be difficult for some entrepreneurs.

It is important to know the differences between the two ways of funding education. For example, getting a bank loan means you will pay the same interest rate over time, helping with financial budgeting. Yet, banks may require entrepreneurs to submit financial forecasts and a complete business plan as part of their loan application. On the other side, having more flexible terms may help, but rising expectations for quick growth and rewards can put pressure on businesses.

It is important to put together a well-structured business plan and deck for pitching your ideas to potential funders. Pointing out estimated income and profit margins in your application can make it more attractive. Being able to explain the market conditions and the company's place among competitors boosts investors' faith in the company.

The process starts with finding investors who are interested in the same goals as those of the business. When possible partners are found, talks start about the equity exchange and the rules for investing. It is important to give this phase careful thought and sometimes get legal advice to guarantee balanced and good agreements for everyone.

It is important to put together a thorough financial plan when researching funding options. It is important to plan for the start-up expenses, future cash flow, and any extra money you may need in unpredictable cases. Using samples and templates can guide you step by step in making a solid financial plan.

For a company to obtain funds, financial forecasting is extremely important. Assuming future income and costs based on data allows entrepreneurs to present a believable prediction of their future growth for investors. Scenario analysis can be used with these forecasts, helping make necessary changes depending on what is happening in the market.

It is important to keep managing finances once the business receives funding to keep going. Taking steps to arrange regular meetings to review finances and work with accounting software can help monitor how things are going financially. Being prepared helps maintain faith in the organization and moves it in a direction that lasts and grows.

All in all, coming up with funding solutions needs careful thought that matches urgent expenses with the business's goals over time. By having a clear view of the good and bad sides of business funding, making highly attractive applications, and practicing careful financial management, entrepreneurs can move through the challenging world of business funding more confidently.

Crafting a Financial Plan

A financial plan acts as the foundation that holds up your entire business venture. The first step is to clearly understand a financial plan, which lays out a detailed approach for a business to use its money to accomplish its goals. This means preparing a budget for starting the business, projecting how much cash will move in and out, and deciding on goals for the company's finances.

A key aspect is to budget the money needed to start the business. It is important to forecast the initial expenses that come with starting a business, including buying equipment, finding an office, and doing initial marketing. Good budgeting helps the entrepreneur avoid surprises and spend time growing the business rather than worrying about money.

It is also key to make projections for cash flow. By using these estimates, businesses can know how much cash is coming in and going out and how the business may perform financially in the future. Cash flow analysis gives a company insight into staying ahead of any liquidity problems and covering all its required payments. You should also make preparations for seasons with lower income and financially shocking surprises.

Financial forecasting is considered a critical skill that all entrepreneurs should have. This process includes using past data and market signs to estimate both future revenue and costs. Thinking in advance allows the company to make good financial decisions and plan for the future. Using different scenarios, companies can assess the impact of unexpected results and be ready for different kinds of market conditions.

Supplying templates for financial statements helps entrepreneurs to picture their financial strategies. These tools let you create an orderly record of your income, expenses, and money flow so you can see how you are doing financially as time goes by. Using samples of financial statements makes it possible to verify and capture crucial financial data accurately.

Ensuring that financial review schedules exist is stressed to maintain good financial control. Reviewing finances routinely helps business owners monitor their profitability, make necessary changes, and guide the company toward meeting its set goals. The use of accounting software helps by automating many of the tasks that are part of financial management.

In the end, ways to handle and follow financial matters are talked about. It covers organizing systems for checking financial results, using systems to keep track of money coming in and going out, and making sure your records are always up-to-date. Having a clear idea of the financial situation allows businesses to decide on improvements that help them grow and remain sustainable.

Overall, the main goal of a financial plan is to help protect and improve a business's financial well-being. Planning for what's ahead, making use of practical resources, and keeping an eye on finances allow the business to meet difficulties and gain profit when it sees opportunities.

CHAPTER 5

BUILDING YOUR BRAND

Defining Brand Identity

At the core of any successful business is a clear brand identity, which goes further than just a logo or a catchy tagline and actually becomes part of what the company stands for. This identity helps steer and shape every business choice and meeting with customers, making sure that every interaction with them reflects what the brand stands for. A robust brand identity isn't just about how our brand looks; it also comes down to how people feel when they see or think about our brand. It includes the spirit, beliefs, and promise that a business tries to show people who are interested in it.

The journey to defining a brand identity starts by having a business think about what it stands for and what makes it stand out from others. These values are at the heart of the brand, showing what the company believes in and what it hopes to do. They also help people make choices, shaping things like what products to make and how to treat customers.

A significant aspect of brand identity is making sure that the company's message is simple and gives people a good idea of what it does. This message should speak to the people the brand is trying to reach, explaining simply and clearly what the brand is all about and why it matters to them. The development of this message needs us to really know what people want, what they are looking for, and what they may find hard so that the brand makes sense to them and talks in a way they'll get and like.

Visual elements are really important for brand identity because they show what the brand stands for and what it wants to say to people. This includes making a logo, picking out some colors that match and look good, and choosing the type of font for the website. Each of these things should be worked on carefully so they show what the brand is really like and help the brand stand out from others.

Besides what you see, the sound and style a brand uses are very important as well. They influence how a brand talks to its customers on different media and websites. A brand's identity is reinforced when its message and overall values are communicated consistently in writing, talking, and visuals. By acting in the same way, brands gain the trust of customers, who keep coming back for what they know to expect from the brand.

This prevents inconsistency across all the channels your company uses. These guidelines help everyone producing content for the brand ensure everything follows the brand's identity. It involves standards for using the company logo, colors, fonts, and also the tone of speech used in communications.

Having a clear and identifiable brand identity achieves much more than just making a business recognizable against competitors. It builds an emotional link with the customer. This results in customers being loyal and enthusiastic about the brand, so they buy its products and tell others about it. With so many options available these days, having a distinct brand helps the business draw in customers and keep them, making it likely for the company to keep gaining success and growing.

Developing Online Presence

Having a strong presence on the internet is now a must for businesses to survive and thrive. Small businesses benefit from the digital world by gaining more customers, connecting with their audience, and building a valuable brand. The first thing to do is to identify the key values and message of the brand. Such work builds a strong brand identity that can be clearly seen in every online effort and material.

Having a logo, matching colors, and a unique typeface is important for helping people remember your brand. All these visual parts should display the same traits and values for the brand in every place online. Keeping the brand's tone and words on point helps people identify with the brand and feel more comfortable with it. A style guide should be created to direct how the brand talks on different digital channels so that everything is consistent.

For any business aiming to be online, a dynamic website is very important. The design should work well and keep users involved at all times. A well-designed site should cater to people viewing it on a mobile device, be easy to explore, and include engaging buttons to lead users to the next step. It is important to follow basic SEO tips to increase your website's visibility in search engines and draw in free traffic. It means learning about keywords, using the right SEO practices on the page, and editing meta tags and descriptions.

The user's experience (UX) is very important for keeping people on a website. It is important that a website loads quickly is easy to navigate, and gives its visitors the information they seek. Using analytics helps businesses track how well the website is performing and spot areas to improve so that it continues to support business objectives.

Social media platforms give businesses a simple and easy way to connect with their customers and get their message out. Selecting the right platforms that match your audience and what your business wants to achieve is really important. Each platform has its way of working and is used by different types of people, so companies have to create different types of content for each one. Creating interesting and easy-to-share content, like pictures and posts that people can interact with, can really help get more people interested in your brand and help you reach more people.

Developing a social media calendar helps you plan out your posts ahead of time so you always have something new and interesting to share. Active engagement with the audience by responding to comments, sending messages, and running live sessions helps people feel like they are part of a group and makes them more loyal to the brand. Additionally, content marketing and blogging give brands a way to show they know what they're talking about and help them connect with the people who read their posts. Identifying common topics and key areas that match the brand and what your audience likes can help you make useful and interesting blog posts.

Incorporating multimedia elements like videos and infographics can make your content easier to understand and more interesting for people to look at. Optimizing content for SEO can make it easier for people to find your website and help bring more visitors to your site. Email marketing is still a powerful way to connect with and keep building good relationships with your customers. Growing an email list by adding lead magnets and putting opt-in forms on your website, personalizing the messages you send, and setting up some automated processes are important ways to help email marketing work well.

Analyzing digital marketing metrics helps you see how well your efforts are doing and lets you make changes if things aren't working out. By picking out important measurements like website traffic, social media engagement, and number of leads, businesses can see how well their online efforts are working and use real data to keep making their online spaces better. In this digital age, having a good presence online means more than just being seen; it's about really making a difference and connecting with people, building a real connection with the audience.

Leveraging Social Media

Social media is a useful tool in small business development that helps increase a business's profile and better connect with potential customers. Starting a small business today means understanding the central role that social media has in marketing. When used properly, these platforms allow small companies to increase their size, relate to their target audience, and have a strong presence on the internet.

Understanding the types of social media platforms the audience is on is the first phase of ineffective usage. Every social media site caters to a different group of people and types of content. For example, visual appeal on Instagram is popular with younger users, while LinkedIn is useful for business-minded professionals. By knowing these differences, companies can adjust their plans to support the one-of-a-kind features and people of each social network.

Sharing interesting and captivating information draws in and helps to maintain the interest of possible customers. Every post and piece of content should reach out to readers so they want to get involved and spread the word. This means including pictures and videos with hard-hitting stories that line up well with the brand's message. Providing content that is both interesting and helpful to readers allows businesses to develop a community that remains loyal to their brand.

Developing a schedule for your social media messages will ensure they are posted at the right time. With this calendar, businesses can arrange their posts, ensuring they always stay active on the Internet.

These tools are very useful because they handle the scheduling process so that your content reaches the audience at the best time.

It is important to get the audience involved in the performance. Promptly answering the messages and comments customers leave can help build a community feeling and reveal that what they say is taken seriously. Arranging live QandA sessions and interactive polls gives audience members a way to interact with each other in real time.

Analyzing social media metrics lets us see how well our tactics are doing. Using analytics tools helps a business check its performance in terms of its level of reach, how users engage, and whether users follow through with purchases. In this way, strategies can be adjusted, and efforts focus on what the business and its audience want and need.

Besides, promotional tools on social media platforms can be used to gain more attention and expand your audience. Paying for promotion allows the business to make sure that its story is shown to the group that is most likely to respond. This approach leads to the highest return because money and attention are focused on the segments that are probably most interested in buying.

Using social media as part of a small business's marketing needs careful consideration and planning. When businesses get to know the unique features of the platforms, make their posts exciting, keep the audience interested, and check analytics, they make the best use of social media. This boosts the business brand, increases interaction with customers, and facilitates small business growth and achievement.

Content Marketing Strategies

Today's business world sees content marketing as a guiding light for small businesses hoping to stand out. This strategy is very important as it helps businesses make their key messages known and interact with their audience. Creating useful, relevant, and consistent content is at the heart of content marketing, as it attracts and holds onto a well-defined audience who, in turn, are likely to make profitable actions.

One of the main elements of successful content marketing is knowing what your audience wants and likes. Businesses need to spend time knowing who their target customers are in order to personalize their content for them. You will need to build detailed profiles of your users to include their demographic information, routines, and things they like. Using these personas allows us to shape content in a way that meets the audience's needs and makes them feel appreciated.

With the audience understood, developing a content strategy that matches the goals of the business becomes the next task. It is important to set out the content to be developed, the channels to use, and how often it will be shared. Marketers can meet the needs of different people and help them stay engaged by including blog posts, videos, infographics, and podcasts. Any content generated should lastingly affect the audience by educating them, providing entertainment or motivation, and gently pointing them toward the business's products or services.

One important factor in content marketing is making sure the publications come out regularly. Using a content calendar can greatly help with achieving consistency. It allows companies to prepare and plan their content, meaning their fans are engaged with new content on a consistent basis. Regularly posting helpful content helps a business gain trust and get noticed by search engines, which supports drawing in new customers.

Engagement is also a key component of content marketing. Sharing information is not enough; Enterprises should interact with customers to encourage trust and loyalty among them. One can achieve this by answering comments, hosting live QandA sessions, and supporting user-made content. Keeping a communication line open lets businesses understand what their audience likes so the business can plan its content accordingly.

Optimizing your content for search engines is key to making the most of your content marketing. You should include suitable keywords in your content, write good meta descriptions, and confirm your website is both friendly to visitors and suitable for mobile browsing. Strong SEO will make the business's content easier to see online, attract additional visitors, and help the website turn those visitors into customers.

Evaluating how successful content marketing has been should not be overlooked. Tracking website traffic, the rate at which users interact, and how many purchases were made gives a clear picture of a content strategy's outcome. Looking at these metrics helps companies understand their strengths and weaknesses, letting them improve their actions for even better outcomes.

In all, content marketing gives little businesses the opportunity to market their brand, relate to their customers, and help the business expand. If they pay attention to who their audience is, give them something worthwhile, and keep up with interactions, companies can build a dedicated following that helps them succeed in the long run.

Email Marketing Techniques

In the realm of digital marketing, email is still a really important tool, giving businesses an easy way to reach their customers. Crafting an effective email marketing strategy means you need to get to know both the simple details of how emails are sent and how to come up with content that's actually interesting and useful.

The foundation of a good email marketing campaign is to get and take care of a strong email list. This begins with putting together good lead magnets, like e-books, webinars, or special offers, that encourage visitors to join the list. Putting sign-up forms in the right places on your website and social media can really help get more people subscribed. Once the list is established, it's time to make sure people stay interested by sharing messages and posts that fit their interests.

Segmentation is key in making sure your emails are interesting and helpful to every kind of subscriber you have. By grouping their customers based on things like age, what they buy, or how active they are, businesses can send messages that actually connect with each person. This approach not only makes the content more interesting and useful for the reader but also boosts the chances that people will take action and buy or do something after reading it. Personalized subject lines and messages can help people open and click on your emails more and make your business feel more connected to the readers.

Automation makes email marketing much easier and quicker for businesses to send out their emails. Setting up automated emails, like welcome messages, reminders for things people left in their cart, or birthday messages, helps Thematic stay in touch with subscribers without forgetting to send important messages on time. These automated workflows give marketers more time to focus on other important tasks and still help keep in touch regularly with the audience. Tools like Mailchimp or HubSpot let you set up automated processes that can be changed to match what your marketing goals are.

Reviewing the results of your email campaigns helps improve them over time. Information such as open rates, click-through numbers, and conversions helps us learn what the audience likes and what should be improved. Testing out various elements in an email can help you better understand your subscribers' likes and behavior. Because of this, marketers are better able to fine-tune their plans and increase the success of their next campaigns.

It is also very important that the emails are attractive and have valuable content. The message in an email should be brief and aligned with the brand, and the text should be clear and nicely designed to be read easily. Adding images, videos, or infographics can help the content stand out and be remembered by readers. The main goal is to place the call-to-action in a clear spot so that recipients can easily complete the desired step, be it purchasing, registering for an event, or accessing the website.

Compliance with regulations such as the General Data Protection Regulation (GDPR) and the CAN-SPAM Act is a vital step. The laws detail how companies may collect and use email addresses, insisting on clear permission from subscribers and offering clear ways to opt-out. Ensuring you follow these guidelines keeps a company safe from lawsuits and builds confidence among the audience.

All in all, email marketing skills depend on coming up with strategies, engaging content, and strongly analyzing the results. When companies work on creating a quality email list, personalizing their messages, using automation, and regularly looking at results, they can get the most out of email marketing for growth and interest.

CHAPTER 6

SETTING UP OPERATIONS

Selecting Technology Tools

Choosing the right technology is vital for any small business owner trying to improve how efficiently the company operates. The procedure requires studying the company's operations and making sure the chosen tools align perfectly with them. You should first closely analyze the main activities that fuel the business. Strong communication tools help keep a team informed, and top-quality financial management software guarantees that the financial status of the business stays on track.

It is necessary to check the scalability and the way the tools can be integrated when choosing new technologies. Over time, a business will require more technology, which needs to be flexible and adapt to its expansion. It is important that the tools are simple to use and that customer support is available so the business can use them today and in the future by every team member.

Moving to the cloud can make a business much more flexible and accessible. Today's geographically spread workplace makes cloud technology important since workers can easily access their business data from anywhere. You can easily use Google Drive or Dropbox to store and access files safely, and QuickBooks Online can make managing your finances easier.

Respecting data and privacy is important when choosing what technology to use. Securing business data at all times matters a lot, and using tools like encryption and two-factor authentication is essential to avoid any breaches.

Specially designed project management techniques for smaller teams help to enhance further how a business operates. Using different project management approaches, for example, Agile or Kanban, helps improve the efficiency of working on projects. When using Trello or Asana, managers can easily assign tasks and check their progress to monitor important milestones and performance.

Strong team communication forms the basis for running a project effectively. Arranging daily stand-ups or joining communication tools such as Slack helps team members work together and communicate, which improves the success of the project. Checking on the progress of projects by using Gantt charts and KPIs keeps them on schedule and connected with what the business wants to achieve.

To sum up, it's important to pick technology tools that fit the business today and can also support its development moving forward. Small business owners can help their teams succeed by making sure the tools they provide are scalable, easy to use, and safe for use. Bringing technology into business operations improves how things are done and makes the company more likely to succeed overall.

Implementing Project Management

The success of any business venture, especially one being run by a small team, depends on good project management. It means using a planned method to carry out and complete projects, meeting all objectives within the given limits. Usually, time, cost, and scope make up the main constraints. The main tasks in project management are controlling risks, managing resources well, and providing quality deliverables, tasks that are necessary for businesses with little to work with.

Taking care of the correct methodology is the primary task in good project management. Every methodology within project management brings something special to the process. When projects need to be flexible and change often, Agile methodologies suit them best. With regular changes happening, Agile is a good choice for companies where things change a lot. Additionally, the Waterfall approach is suited to projects that can be structured stage by stage and where changes are limited once work starts. Thanks to its visual system for organizing tasks, Kanban makes it simple to keep track of the status of work, which is great for teams that need to see things at a glance.

If project management software is used, tasks related to managing projects can be done much more efficiently. Both Trello and Asana include resources to help managers distribute assignments, track deadlines, and review how work is moving forward. They ensure teams work openly and honestly and are all working towards the same project goals. Using these tools on a daily basis can help organize time and make better use of resources.

Clear communication forms a key part of successful project management. With effective communication, team members can all understand what is happening and identify fewer mistakes. Holding brief daily meetings ensures everyone stays updated on what is happening with others. With the help of tools like Slack, communication can happen instantly, and more information can be shared with the team.

Monitoring how the project is coming along helps keep the project on track. By marking key milestones and using Gantt charts and KPIs, it becomes simpler to see if progress is on track according to the plan. With these tools, managers can see how the project is progressing and make interventions if anything goes off schedule.

Consequently, introducing project management in a small business setting requires proper selection of methodology, proper use of the tools, maintaining effective communication, and frequently monitoring achievements. As a result, small businesses are able to handle their projects better, ensuring that everything is done properly, on schedule, and at the right cost. It supports the business in achieving its goals and also supports its growth and future.

Enhancing Team Communication

Teams in small businesses must communicate well together for the company to thrive. The way individuals communicate in a company determines the speed of work, the atmosphere at work, and the overall results. Clear channels of open communication help achieve business goals and also support the company's progress.

Connecting effectively as a team is possible after identifying useful communication tools and choosing the ones that best match the team. Using technology such as this, people can now video conferencing, message instantly, or work together online. With these tools, communication and collaboration can happen fast, and information is available in real-time, no matter where team members are located. Yet, the software to use ought to reflect what the business needs, team members' tastes, and dependability.

Other than using available technology, making dialogue important and encouraging people to share their thoughts is key to improving communication. It means that the setting allows everyone to share their thoughts, raise concerns, and give comments. Having regular meetings gives everyone a chance to talk openly so that all work efforts stay aligned. The meetings should have a set structure, but be willing to respond to any creative ideas that arise during the day.

The most important aspect of any message is being clear. If messages are simple and clear, everyone on the team knows what is expected of them. Establishing project management tools helps all parties see what their roles are in the project and the deadlines they have to meet. You can use charts and diagrams as visual tools to help explain data and processes more clearly.

Although we talk a lot, just listening can be equally important in communication. Knowing that others are listening to them encourages each person in the team to respect and trust their colleagues. It guarantees that every person's input is taken into account, which can improve the way decisions are made and how the group works together. Teaching team members proper listening skills can help them get the most out of their relationships at work.

No communication improvement is sustainable unless feedback keeps coming in. Regular communication between the team ensures they can comment on what works or doesn't in the current model and set improvements in place. This can be managed by using anonymous surveys, suggestion boxes, or open forums. It is important that feedback targets how things can be done better, as well as improves the team's overall effectiveness.

When resources are not abundant in a small business, effective communication can boost both work productivity and employee morale. It supports cooperation, new ideas, and the ability to bounce back. Strong communication helps businesses improve their day-to-day operations and puts them in good standing to meet new challenges in a dynamic market.

Time Management Strategies

Managing time well is a must in entrepreneurship, where things happen quickly. Having a lot to do can cause entrepreneurs to juggle many tasks at the same time, so managing time wisely is key.

Many people find it helpful to set aside work for 25 minutes and take a very short pause between each of their 25-minute work blocks. This method not only improves your ability to stay focused but also prevents you from becoming tired. Using the Eisenhower Matrix, entrepreneurs can organize duties in order of importance, using this as a guide for what to prioritize.

Prioritization is what makes time management work well. Entrepreneurs need to establish and keep top priorities. They should make sure their daily tasks help meet the long-term aims of the business. An individual must make a priority list to judge which activities are most important and should be worked on first. Doing what is important for the company's objectives helps entrepreneurs move their business ahead.

Productivity tools are very important when it comes to managing your time. Using Todoist and calendar tools can greatly help boost company organization and schedule projects. Using these tools, people can manage their deadlines by scheduling meetings and appointments.

Establishing and keeping up with daily routines can help people become more productive. Developing regular morning and evening routines is a good way to start your day calmly and relax at the end of it. Moreover, separating work from personal time helps avoid becoming too tired and maintain a good balance between the two. To do this, make sure to plan set times for your career and personal affairs to keep each separate from the other.

Using a lean approach in business is one way to help with time management. Using lean principles, entrepreneurs can limit what they spend on and focus on what brings the most value to their business. Having an agile mindset makes the team more flexible and ready to adapt to both changing market trends and what their customers say.

On top of organizing themselves, team leaders can free up a lot of time for main responsibilities by sharing duties with their staff. Entrepreneurs need to choose tasks that others can take care of so they can focus on important business decisions.

All in all, effective time management for entrepreneurs uses different strategies and tools to boost their productivity and efficiency. Using strategies such as the Pomodoro Technique or the Eisenhower Matrix, productivity tools, consistent habits, and keeping the business lean and agile let entrepreneurs control their time and grow their company successfully. This way of planning helps the business reach its instant goals while preparing for future achievements.

Building Lean Business Models

Striving for a lean business model helps small businesses achieve success. With a lean model, companies try to achieve the greatest value for customers with the minimum amount of wasted resources. The method is useful for small businesses because the ability to react quickly can determine whether they will succeed or fail.

In lean business models, businesses are always looking to improve through continuous change, known as Kaizen. Doing so requires checking and updating the way things are done in order to remove inefficiencies and improve what they achieve. Businesses that always look for ways to improve are more likely to keep up with changing customer demands and trends. Recurring checks will find and eliminate non-essential activities, making operations more effective and economical.

Building a Minimum Viable Product (MVP) is also very important. An MVP is used by a business to test its main functions in the market with as little effort and expense as possible. This strategy saves resources and gives important insights into what people want and what the market is looking for. By asking early users for their opinions, businesses learn what types of improvements and new features might be needed, helping to keep customer needs met with each new release.

Customer feedback loops play a vital part in lean manufacturing, allowing users to share their views on satisfaction and what needs fixing. The information from this feedback helps the company continue to improve its products so they satisfy the needs of its customers. Listening to what customers say allows businesses to create features that improve their satisfaction and enjoyment of the product, thus boosting their loyalty to the company.

In addition, lean business models support having an adaptable company structure that can move quickly in response to changes. It means creating an environment that inspires everyone to be creative and to try out new solutions. When employees are allowed to propose new ideas and test them, teams' creative power can encourage innovation. The focus on experimentation brings about new answers to problems and encourages the team to feel engaged.

Partnerships are also key to building a lean business model. Partnering with other companies allows businesses to reach new markets, benefit from new technologies, and learn from their experience, benefiting customers. These partnerships may be in the form of ventures, shared brands, or common use of resources, and all have their positives when trying to maximize value and minimize cost.

In the end, lean business models stress that scaling should still happen while maintaining high quality. As businesses grow, keeping up the quality of their products and services is really important for keeping their customers' trust and loyalty. For this reason, strong quality control and the ability to expand must be present in the industry. By putting in place standard ways of doing things and using helpful tools, businesses can keep making good products or services as they grow and serve more people.

In short, a lean business model is built by working on efficiency, managing changes, and providing value. By using lean principles, small businesses can get better at handling tough times, make more customers happy, and keep growing in a tough market.

CHAPTER 7

SALES AND CUSTOMER RELATIONS

Understanding Sales Process

In the realm of small business, the sales process is really important because it helps bring in money, makes customers happier, and helps businesses keep good relationships with people over time. Understanding the sales process is really important for any new business owner because it helps set up how to talk to customers and grow the business.

The sales process starts when the company finds people who might be interested in what it has to offer. This step means figuring out who or what might find your products or services useful, whether they are people, businesses, or other organizations. It requires studying the market well and really getting to know the audience so you can figure out where people interested in your product or service are usually found. This stage is important because it helps build a good foundation for all the other things that come after.

Once you know who your potential leads are, the next thing to do is reach out and start a conversation. This means talking to people through emails, calls, social media, or even meeting in person. The goal is to build some trust and start a conversation that helps the business get to know what the customer needs and how the business can help meet those needs. Effective communication skills are important here because they help explain what your product or service can do in a way that makes it easy to understand and want to get.

Following the initial contact, the process then starts with checking that the company really matches what the buyer is looking for. This step is about figuring out if the lead is likely to move forward and thus might be worth spending more time on. It means looking at how likely a lead is to buy something by checking things like how interested they are, how much money they can spend, and when they might want to make a purchase. This step helps you pick which leads are most likely to become customers and focus on them so you don't waste time on people who are less likely to buy.

At this point, the entrepreneur demonstrates the product or service by outlining its benefits and how it helps the customer. During this step, it is possible to emphasize what fits the lead's requirements and situation best in the presentation. Dealing with any questions the lead may have helps to establish trust and confidence in what is being offered.

After all the talks, the main goal becomes agreeing on an arrangement suitable for both sides. You need to talk about pricing terms and address any objections the lead might mention. Good negotiation may help satisfy the business and the customer without causing misunderstanding. You need to be patient and persistent and always keep in mind what the customer wants to succeed in closing a sale.

After a payment is received, there are still things to take care of. Follow-up after the purchase is necessary to check if the customer is happy and to deal with any problems they encounter. It is at this point that companies begin to form lasting connections and generate more regular orders. Gathering feedback from the audience can greatly improve the quality of offered products and services.

The main aim of learning the sales process is to build trust with your customers and deliver what they need. All steps, starting from getting leads and ending with follow-up, help create a positive customer experience and contribute to business achievements. Building these abilities can allow a small business to grow in sales, gain loyal clients, and sustain its progress.

Building Customer Relationships

A small business can only thrive when it forms good relationships with its customers. Having good relationships in the market can play a big role in making customers stay loyal and help a business succeed over the long haul. Knowing how to communicate with customers and provide a personal touch are important for achieving this.

Building trust and being dependable are important to building a customer relationship. Businesses should always deliver what they have promised so that their products and services are as good as customers expect them to be. Because the business is reliable, customers feel confident in using it again and are likely to suggest it to someone else. Being upfront about what your product or service can do, as well as its restrictions, is also very important. When clients trust a business, it's because the business is upfront with it.

If you want strong relations with your customers, you need to pay close attention to what they have to say. It is important for businesses to regularly get feedback by communicating with customers through surveys and conversations online and in person. A feedback loop makes it possible to learn about customer wants and needs and also helps customers understand that their opinion is valued. Making improvements based on customer opinions can improve satisfaction and underline the company's desire never to stop bettering itself.

Making customer relationships more personal brings about many advantages. Changing products, services, and communications according to each customer's needs often improves how customers feel. Sending personalized deals or recommendations with customer data allows the business to prove its values and care about its customers, which can build a stronger bond with them. As a result, personalization can make customers more loyal and likely to spread positive word-of-mouth.

Furthermore, businesses should try to give customers experiences they'll remember so their brand stays in people's minds. These experiences can include things like getting really good customer help or finding products that no one else sells. By going above what people expect and offering something extra, businesses can make a strong impact on their customers and keep them coming back.

Developing a customer-centric culture in the business is very important. Employees should be taught how important it is to keep customers happy and given the authority to make choices that make things better for people who buy from the company. This culture of customer focus needs to happen at every level of the company so that every time a customer interacts with the business, they feel that the company really cares about their needs.

In addition to talking to customers face-to-face, businesses also use things like online chat, customer feedback forms, and social media to better connect with their customers. Social media platforms, email marketing, and CRM systems help companies connect with customers, learn what their needs are, and offer things that better fit what each customer wants. These tools help businesses keep in touch with their customers all the time, making sure they stay up-to-date and interested in what the brand is doing.

Ultimately, building good relationships with customers means coming up with a plan that uses trust, getting to know their needs, listening to what they say, and always putting them first. By building trust and giving customers great service, businesses can create a group of regular customers who keep buying from them and even help bring in new ones. This foundation of strong relationships helps small businesses do well and keeps them growing when things in the market are changing.

Developing a Pricing Strategy

A good pricing strategy starts by analyzing the market, keeping track of your costs, and making sure it matches your business goals. A good pricing strategy is built upon a detailed analysis of the market. This means you should figure out who your target customers are and note their interests, ways of buying, and responses to changes in the price they pay. It is important to conduct a competitive analysis as well. Comparing the prices of similar items from competitors will allow you to figure out how to make your offerings different. This analysis points out any gaps in the market where your pricing strategy has a chance to work.

After understanding the market context, you should look into the financial aspects of your business. It is important to calculate the costs related to making and delivering your product or service accurately. Knowing your fixed and variable expenses will help you pick a price that covers those costs and leaves space for a profit that fits your business's goals. You should take into account the costs of materials and labor as well as other indirect expenses such as overhead and administration.

Once market conditions and costs are understood, picking the right pricing model becomes the next step. You can choose from several different types of business models according to your type of business and market status. A company sets its prices this way by charging more than the original cost of the goods to guarantee it can turn a profit. Additionally, value-based pricing measures how much the customer values the product rather than counting the cost. Markets where being unique and different are important are where this typically succeeds.

Another important part of pricing strategy is using what people call psychological pricing, which means making choices about things like how prices are shown or how often sales happen to try to get customers to buy more. This means putting prices in a way that grabs peoples' attention, like charging $9.99 instead of $10, since it can affect how people see a product and how much they decide to spend. Additionally, pricing strategies can involve things like giving special discounts or running temporary sales to encourage people to buy during certain times.

Equally important is having the ability to adjust prices depending on what the market needs. Markets are always moving and changing, as people want different things, and businesses try to stay ahead of each other. Hence, it is important to check and update your pricing plans from time to time so your business can keep up and reach its goals. This might include things like making changes in line with the seasons, reacting to what other brands are doing, or adjusting based on changes in how much it costs to make products.

Finally, your customers must know about your pricing, so let people know about how much things cost. The way you show prices to customers can really affect how they see what you're selling and what they end up choosing to buy. Clear communication of why your product is worth the money helps people understand why it's priced that way and makes them happier and more loyal to your business. Additionally, making sure your sales team can clearly share pricing information and handle any questions or pushback about prices is important for making sure your pricing plan actually works in the market.

In summary, coming up with a pricing strategy takes into account how the market is working, what it costs to make or deliver a product, and what customers think about the price. By picking the best pricing option for their business and staying flexible, companies can help set themselves up well in the market, get more sales, and reach their financial goals.

Handling Customer Feedback

Any small business owner needs to be skilled in dealing with customer feedback. It is important to recognize clients' needs, make products or services better, and ensure happiness with what is received. Firms need to design a consistent system for seeking out feedback. Firms often conduct surveys, use feedback forms, or interview customers to find out what they think. The way you design the methods matters so they give us truthful and comprehensive answers using both types of data.

When all the feedback is gathered, the following step is to look at this information carefully. The feedback is broken down into themes to help recognize any repeated issues or suggestions. Analytics helps businesses turn qualitative comments into measurable data, allowing them to understand what customers are thinking more clearly. It should help discover trends and patterns to assist in making appropriate decisions. The focus should be on giving priority to feedback depending on its frequency, whether it is urgent, and how much impact it might have on the business.

Following up on feedback and making improvements is how businesses show they are committed to customers. This means you have to turn feedback into improvements you can put into practice. Every improvement to a product, support process, or finding a solution to a common issue should be guided by the company's strategies. To implement changes successfully, different departments need to come together to ensure that everything is well-integrated into business processes.

Responding to customer feedback relies heavily on communication. It is important to inform customers about how their feedback is being used to help them feel included and valued. Regular updates are possible by publishing newsletters, sharing on social media, or getting in touch with customers personally. Telling customers what you do with their feedback can help them trust the company more and feel appreciated.

Additionally, it is necessary to create a workplace that accepts and values feedback. Getting employees to communicate with customers can lead to a business that is more focused on them. Training all staff to manage criticism, both negative and positive, is extremely crucial. Allowing employees to solve problems quickly and well helps avoid negative feelings and makes room for growth on both sides.

Making sure there is a feedback loop helps the system grow over time. This needs managers to frequently check and fine-tune the feedback processes to maintain their value and usefulness. If businesses regularly obtain and work with customer opinions, they can both make their services better and form good relationships with their customers. Having a proactive approach sets a business apart in the market and shows that it truly values what its customers think and feel.

Creating Loyalty Programs

For small businesses competing to survive, having loyal customers is necessary, as it helps a lot in the long run. They work as ways for businesses to keep customers by offering perks and creating loyalty to the brand. A successful loyalty program gives true value to customers and supports what the business aims to achieve.

There are many types of loyalty programs designed for different kinds of businesses and what their customers want. These programs are mainly created to encourage customers to come back for another purchase with rewards that appeal to them. For example, in a points system, every purchase customers make nets them points that can be used for discounts or free items later. By using this method, businesses get people to keep buying and staying engaged with the brand due to the sign-up bonus.

Offering tiered loyalty also helps companies reward their customers with different rewards tied to their level of purchases. It leads to higher spending and creates a more special experience for the customer. These kinds of programs work especially well for businesses trying to build a stronger link with their clients. Status and community factors entice customers to move up and reach better tiers.

More people are signing up for loyalty programs that use subscriptions, mainly when they buy from companies that offer repeat purchases. Such programs usually offer their members regular benefits like free shipping and opportunities to buy products first but require a regular membership fee. It not only gives the business a continuous income but also helps customers relate more closely to the brand.

A loyalty program will only work if it is relevant and easy to use. It is important to design the program so that it appeals to the unique tastes and actions of the chosen audience. This calls for a detailed knowledge of customer groups and how they make purchases, both of which are possible with data analytics. When businesses use customer information to personalize rewards, the program becomes more interesting and successful.

The success of loyalty programs greatly depends on good communication. Updating customers on their rewards, benefits, and upcoming perks helps to engage them and encourages them to join in more. Using email, mobile apps, and social media together makes sure that the information is delivered to where customers spend most of their time.

On top of this, loyalty programs give businesses the chance to understand their customers' actions better. After studying the data collected, companies can update their marketing methods, adjust their line of products, and achieve higher growth.

Yet, planning and executing a loyalty program are both important steps to take. Businesses need to ensure that the rewards are profitable and that the program works well with the rest of the customer experience. Keeping the program updated and relevant is important so that customers' needs and expectations are met as they change.

Making a loyalty program is not only about giving out discounts or promotions. By focusing on customers, supporting a community, and creating something people are proud of, brands can thrive. In this way, businesses are able to build lasting relationships with customers and gain an edge over others in their sector.

Make a Difference with Your Review

Title:
Starting A Small Business
Unlock the Power of Generosity

"Success is not final; failure is not fatal: It is the courage to continue that counts." — Winston Churchill

People who give without expecting anything back often live the happiest lives. That's why I'm asking for a small but powerful favor from you.

Would you help someone just like you — someone eager to start **Starting A Small Business** but unsure where to begin?

My goal is to make starting and growing a small business simple, practical, and achievable for everyone who needs it. But to reach more people, I need your help.

Most readers choose a book based on reviews. So, by writing just a few kind words, you could help someone take the first step toward change.

Your quick review could help:
• One more person find clarity and focus.
• One more beginner feel confident about starting.
• One more journey toward self-improvement begin.
• One more dream become reality.

To make a difference, just scan the QR code below or visit:
https://a.co/d/egO0Vhp

If you enjoy helping others, you're my kind of person. Thank you so much for your support!

CAMERON BANKS

CHAPTER 8

MANAGING GROWTH

Identifying Expansion Opportunities

For small businesses, spotting opportunities to grow is important to ensure the business thrives and remains successful for many years. This is done by studying the market, looking at what consumers want, and assessing what the business can do so that owners can put their business in the best position for future advancement.

It's important to look at market demand and its readiness when starting to explore expansion opportunities. This step involves doing a market analysis to find out the current level of demand and to detect any trends that may influence the demand in the future. Observing consumer behavior allows companies to see which way opinions are changing and then plan for potential growth in those directions.

Trying out new places as markets can be a meaningful way for a business to expand. Any move into different regions or overseas markets needs thorough preparation and an awareness of the local rules and ways of life. A feasibility study needs to be carried out to understand if the company's products will work in these new markets, allowing it to meet local needs and handle any local rules.

Company expansion can also be achieved by diversifying its line of products or offerings. Looking at how existing products perform allows businesses to create opportunities for additional or new products that will interest different customer groups. It helps a company gain new customers and avoid the risks of depending on a limited range of products.

Strategic partnerships can be useful when it comes to growing the business. Collaboration allows businesses to draw in a wider customer base, improve the products offered, and lower the cost of using resources. Finding ways to work together and co-brand with partners can result in relationships that are good for both parties and help your businesses prosper.

Using customer opinions in product and service design helps to adjust and improve everything to meet customers' new needs. By conducting surveys and focus groups on a regular basis, businesses can know what improvements and changes will matter most to their customers.

It is also important to use technology to help manage and shape new products as a means of identification. With the use of artificial intelligence and the Internet of Things, companies are able to introduce personalized services and stand out from everyone else.

In addition, offering more ways to receive support makes it easier to serve a larger group of people. Offering an online shop or allowing subscription options can make things easier for customers and help the company grow in the market.

Working towards sustainability and social responsibility lets businesses find new ways to progress. When a company uses eco-friendly methods and finds sustainable materials, it becomes appealing to those concerned about the environment and helps build a better brand image.

The ability to respond quickly and remain flexible to changes in the market helps a business find expansion opportunities. Keeping an eye on changes in the industry, responding to what customers want, and using strong partnerships help small businesses continue to grow successfully.

Enhancing Product Offerings

Offering more and different products is important for small businesses to continue to grow and remain ahead of the competition. To achieve this, companies need to use customer opinions, keep up with advances in technology, and use environmentally sound ways.

The initial stage of perfecting the product range involves directly including what customers say in the development process. To decide what to improve next, companies use surveys focus groups, and speak directly to customers to learn what is most important to them. Being customer-focused builds loyalty and ensures the business keeps up with the latest market changes.

The use of new technology is crucial for adding features to a product. By using technology such as AI and the Internet of Things, companies are able to give people unique and intelligent experiences when using products. Due to these innovations, ordinary products can offer much more to customers, helping the business stand out from its competition.

Diversifying how products are delivered to customers is a useful way to add value to the product range. Building an online shopping site or offering services on subscription helps businesses attract more customers and offer them easier ways to buy goods. It helps a company connect with more customers and satisfy them by reaching them directly through new technologies.

It is now more important than ever for businesses to pay attention to sustainability and social responsibility. Taking steps to obtain eco-friendly resources and use green production methods allows businesses to support the environment and satisfy conscious buyers. Being green in business can be an effective way to set a company apart from many others.

Companies should keep coming up with new ideas and changing to stay ahead. This means working on what works well now and also being open to new ideas and chances. Running innovation workshops and putting money into research and development can encourage creativity and result in finding solutions that keep up with changing consumer trends.

Understanding what is happening in the market and how consumers behave is key when applying these strategies. If businesses monitor the market regularly and keep track of changes in their industry, they will have enough time to update their offerings. It allows businesses to stay ahead and build sustainable success over the years.

In the end, providing more products should help customers and put the business ahead of the competition. By using what they learn about their customers, keeping up with advancements in technology, increasing ways to deliver products, and staying committed to sustainability, small businesses can build attractive products and see rising growth.

Utilizing Strategic Partnerships

Having strategic partnerships can be a key reason for a small business to succeed. When set up properly, small businesses have the benefit of increased exposure, improved capabilities, and a way to pursue new markets without massive up-front expenses. Strategic partnerships should be centered on both companies' profit, and they do so by each using what the other is good at to achieve common goals.

The first thing to do in making a strategic partnership is to find possible collaborators who share your objectives. To do this, it is important to know your business needs and the goals you set within your strategy. When you lay out what you are capable of and what resources you have, you can easily see which areas need help or can improve with a partnership. This arrangement can provide new technology, access to other markets, or even team-up on marketing strategies. For example, a bakery teaming up with a coffee shop nearby would allow both companies to advertise each other and get more people through their doors.

When trying to win over a partner, it is important to come up with an attractive value proposition. It should make it clear that both the buyer and the supplier have something to gain from working together. You ought to make sure you understand the business of your potential partner and see how the partnership might work for both sides. In a good proposal, the joined aims, matching principles, and how your businesses add value to each other will be pointed out. This way of thinking strengthens the appeal for the partnership and supports the formation of a lasting relationship.

Good communication must continue once the partnership is set. It is about setting what is expected, defining who does what, and deciding how to handle disagreements or make decisions. Both should agree about what success looks like and how to check progress. Keeping in contact and sharing updates help to make sure that everyone stays on the same track in response to changes in the industry. Having trust and transparency in a partnership is important, and effective communication helps achieve this.

It is very important to put the partnership in writing with a legal agreement. It should detail the conditions of the partnership, including how partners will share responsibilities finances, and for how long the deal will last. It is advisable to seek legal advice to address all areas of the partnership and protect both side's interests. By having a clear agreement, it is easier to solve any problems that arise between the parties.

Continual assessment of how successful the partnership is is an important process. When assessments are done frequently, both parties can look at the partnership objectives and confirm it is meeting the set goals. It is important to use measures of income growth or how involved customers are while also paying attention to intangible factors like teamwork. Honoring achievements and facing challenges when they happen helps enhance the relationship and open doors to future work together.

The goal of these partnerships is to create outcomes that neither organization can achieve working alone. Working together and using each partner's strengths, small businesses are better positioned to innovate and grow more efficiently. With competition sometimes coming second to working together, partnerships provide an effective strategy for small businesses to flourish in a difficult market.

Scaling Operations

When a small business begins to grow, scaling becomes key to keeping up with the expansion and maintaining high quality. For this, it is necessary to have processes and procedures that are always the same. Clearly defined operation manuals and set quality control points ensure that businesses manage consistency in their products even with higher volumes. With these procedures acting as a guideline, it becomes easy for employees to do their work with the same attention to detail and efficiency.

Taking care of staff training and development plays a big role in scaling up effectively. When demands rise, the labor force must be ready to meet the challenges that come with them. Skill-building and leadership programs ensure staff members are up to the new responsibilities. If employees are given the proper education and training, businesses can make sure their standards are maintained as the business continues to grow.

Using automation helps to speed up the scaling of a business. When organizations use robots for routine work and software for automated processes, they become much more efficient. Automation leads to less chance of manual errors and enables human personnel to pay more attention to important tasks. As a result, companies can more efficiently use their employees by making critical parts of the business a priority.

Monitoring quality by looking at important performance measures (KPIs) and running regular audits is very important so that good operations are kept up as the business expands. Setting good KPIs means performance can be measured, and audits frequently help to find places where growth is needed. As a result of regular monitoring, businesses can make changes and ensure that their products or services are always of high quality.

It is also very important to follow new market trends and advancements to grow. Remaining aware of new technology trends and using agile processes allows businesses to respond rapidly to changes in the market. Agile practices, like having teams work together from different areas and using simple project management tools, help the company stay up-to-date with changes in the market, making sure it does well against its competitors.

Experimenting with new ways of doing business and encouraging staff to try out new ideas are both important steps. By trying out new ways of selling products directly to people or by using gig economy services to deliver goods or services, businesses can come up with new ideas and better ways to serve their customers. Building a culture where all mistakes can be used to learn, and new ideas are possible can result in strong business growth.

Building a culture of continuous improvement means getting employees to help with making the business better and setting up simple ways for them to give and get feedback. Allowing changes and improvements to be heard and implemented can keep businesses moving forward and dealing with issues as they come up. Utilizing data analytics to look for issues and ways to get better lets businesses find things that do not work well and come up with simpler and better ways to do things.

Planning for sustainable success also means setting a plan for the future and ensuring there is a trained team ready to take over. Building a strong image and reputation helps a business ensure its expansion plans will continue to be sustainable. Diversifying revenue and saving money help make the business more secure in times of trouble and during economic downturns.

Adapting to Market Trends

In the ever-changing world of business, it's really important that small companies can keep up with what customers want if they want to stay in business and grow. Entrepreneurs must keep an eye out for changes happening in their industry and be ready to change their plans when it's needed. This dynamic approach needs planning, the ability to adapt, and coming up with new ideas to help a business both stay alive and do well when the market changes.

First and foremost, you need to really get to know the market before you start looking for properties. This means checking the market often so you can learn about what customers want, what your competitors are up to, and any new trends. Businesses should use tools like surveys, group talks, and data analysis to figure out what customers want and get ready to meet their needs in the future. By paying close attention to what people are talking about, entrepreneurs can adjust their products or services to fit what their customers really need or want.

Furthermore, staying ahead of the competition means doing more than just keeping an eye on what's popular. People and teams need to be ready to come up with new ideas and always think about how their business can improve. Businesses should create an atmosphere where people are free to be creative and try out new ideas so they can come up with solutions that help the company do better. This can be done by holding idea workshops, bringing people together for brainstorming, and making sure there is money put aside for research and new projects. By making new and better products or services, companies can stand out from the competition and get more customers.

Flexibility is also really important when it comes to keeping up with what the market is doing. Businesses must be ready to change their plans and ways of doing things when things in the market change. This may mean changing how prices are set, switching up advertising, or giving the company a new name just to fit what customers want. Scenario planning can be helpful during this process by letting businesses look at different possible futures and come up with backup plans for what could happen.

Building strong customer relationships also helps businesses keep up with the changes happening in the market. Loyal customers can share helpful input and ideas that can help businesses figure out what to do next. Implementing feedback loops, which involve asking customers for their thoughts and using that information in how the business works, can help make sure that what the company offers is still useful and up-to-date for its customers. Personalized customer experiences and great service can help build customers' trust and make them more likely to stick around and recommend your brand.

Finally, using new technology can really help a business keep up with changes in the market. Technology can help make work run more smoothly, make it easier to connect with customers and find new ways for the business to grow. For instance, using digital marketing tools lets businesses connect with more people, and having an online store can give them more ways to sell their stuff. By using new technology, businesses can do things more efficiently and make sure they are giving their customers what they need.

In conclusion, adapting to market trends means using a mix of things like studying the market, coming up with new ideas, being flexible, coming closer to customers, and using technology. By staying up-to-date and flexible, small businesses can handle changes in the market and look for chances to grow. This proactive stance helps keep the business safe from things that could go wrong and also helps it do well in the future.

CHAPTER 9

FINANCIAL MANAGEMENT

Managing Cash Flow

For a small business to be healthy and sustainable, it needs to understand cash flow. Cash flow measures the incoming and outgoing money of a business and is used to determine its financial stability and capacity to pay bills. Examining a cash flow statement can help business owners see trends and prepare for phases when cash is plentiful or tight. Carrying out this analysis helps a business maintain a positive cash flow to cover its expenses when due.

First, it is important to fully grasp the basics of cash flow statements if you want to control cash flow. They provide a detailed review of the money going into and coming out of the company. With this knowledge, those running a business can anticipate when income will rise or fall and adjust accordingly.

You should also plan for unexpected expenses when managing your cash flow. Setting up an emergency fund could help prepare you for unexpected costs. Planning for potential surprises should form a habit in financial management so that surprises do not threaten the business. This strategy can protect a business from financial difficulties and help it function properly.

The best way to increase positive cash flow is to manage how your company receives and pays its money. Practicing good billing habits can ensure that you always get paid quickly. It is possible to control outflows by securing good payment terms from suppliers. By doing this, both liquidity and business relationships are made stronger.

It is very important to track and predict your cash flow regularly. Through forecasting, owners can determine whether they should have sufficient cash and avoid insufficient funds. They may be as basic as a simple spreadsheet or as advanced as major financial software based on how intricate the business is. Regular meetings to discuss cash flow help the company make quick adjustments to its finances and prevent any financial instability.

When overseeing cash flow, it should be understood that much more is involved than simply watching the numbers. As part of this process, businesses make plans and predictions to meet all their financial duties and find ways to grow. It is important to manage saving and investing so that enough cash is on hand to keep day-to-day activities going, though there is still an opportunity to grow the business.

Good cash flow management allows the business to weather tough times. If a company has positive cash flow, it becomes stronger during ups and downs in the economy and can respond to any new opportunities. The importance of this task in managing finances is that it ensures a small business has enough resources to operate now and in the future. Businesses that pay close attention to cash flow are more likely to prosper even in a tough business environment.

Budgeting Effectively

To succeed, a small business must have a budget that is simple and flexible. To begin, a business owner must have a precise view of the company's finances, showing expected earnings and the expected costs. Begin by spotting all opportunities to make money. You should look at the sales forecast, estimates for services, and any additional sources of income. Estimating the expected revenue accurately helps you decide on goals that are possible to achieve.

While gathering this information, input all the expenses you can expect to have, both those that stay the same and those that change. In most cases, rent, utilities, and staff salaries are consistent throughout the month. Variable costs, such as supplies, money spent on marketing, and travel costs, are all items that can change on a regular basis. When arranging expenses, business leaders can anticipate their cash flow and realize where they may save money.

After summarizing the financial data, the following step is to make a complete budget plan. It is important to have monthly and yearly projections included to support planning now and in the future. Budgeting software or spreadsheets can be very useful as they structure the way you manage and evaluate your budget. It is crucial to revise and examine the budget often so it remains up-to-date with the company's finances.

A good budget should include a plan for unplanned costs. Having an emergency fund ensures that financial shocks do not affect the stability of a company. Start by reserving a small portion of each paycheck until you have accumulated a nice safety net.

Budgeting involves closely watching cash flow as well. With the help of cash flow statements, it's easy to monitor when the company gets paid and pays its bills to keep cash positive. Performing a regular review of these statements can help you spot patterns and recognize upcoming financial needs.

Setting reasonable and tough financial goals is a part of budgeting. They ought to line up with the business's strategy, which could consist of achieving higher sales, better cost control, or boosting profits. When you split your goals into the steps you'll take, it makes it easier to accomplish them.

It is also essential to pay attention to any outside influences that could shape the company's finances. Budgeting plans can be influenced by changes in the market, the economy, or industry regulations. If a company is informed and flexible, it can respond to changes by making budget updates on its terms.

This way, financial discipline within the company means that all workers know how important it is to follow the budget. An example could be mandatory financial checks, putting in place policies, and encouraging all staff to provide ideas for saving money. If the team is involved in budgeting, everyone becomes responsible for the financial well-being of the company.

Overall, budgeting is about more than saving money; it's also about choosing actions that help a company succeed in the long term. It involves being ambitious yet realistic so that funds are placed where they best add value for the business.

Forecasting and Scenarios

The ability to predict and create scenarios plays a major role in determining if a small business will thrive and stay sustainable. Forecasting is about making guesses about upcoming trends using information from the past and the present market. To do this, a person must notice small details and understand the possible effects of signals in the marketplace.

Collecting and reviewing appropriate data should be the main focus when starting forecasting. We may obtain this data by looking at historical sales, doing market research, and studying economic indicators. An analysis of this data allows entrepreneurs to find out what could influence the company's results in the future. Forecasting is not a perfect process; it mainly requires predicting future events using available facts.

As soon as the data is collected and reviewed, you need to create some scenarios. With scenario planning, you can make flexible plans for the future. Various future scenarios are designed to help see both risks and advantages. As a result, businesses are better able to get ready for whatever might unfold as each scenario is considered. Considering different possible outcomes allows businesses to manage risks and take full advantage of opportunities.

Using scenarios in planning helps entrepreneurs respond to issues before they occur. In this scenario, an entrepreneur may order more production or purchase new technology. If an emergency happens and the situation is serious, it may be useful to cut costs or make money come from several sources. Being flexible and changing strategies when needed is key to ensuring the business endures various events.

To ensure forecasts are as accurate as possible, use both quantitative and qualitative methods. Some examples of quantitative methods used in finance are statistical models and financial projections, and some qualitative methods are gathering opinions from experts and checking research studies. Integrating these methods allows businesses to build stronger and more dependable forecasts.

Additionally, technology is an important part of up-to-date forecasting. Through data processing, predictive analytics shows patterns in data that a person might not notice at first. They allow the process to be automated, so it is performed faster and more accurately than manual forecasting.

Frequent revisions to the forecast are necessary as well. If any new data comes out or if the market changes, the forecasts must be updated. It allows the company to adjust its strategies based on the present state of the market.

Communicating the forecasts and scenarios to necessary stakeholders is also very important. It requires breaking down data in a way that makes sense, outlining significant assumptions, and pointing out potential results for the company. When stakeholders are informed and agree with the forecast, a business can implement its strategies easily.

Overall, understanding the process of forecasting and creating scenarios gives small business owners the necessary insight to meet uncertain situations and take advantage of upcoming opportunities. Continuous analysis of data, creating different scenarios, and correctly planning strategies can keep the business operating successfully.

Working with Financial Advisors

Small business management relies greatly on financial advisors. They assist business owners in managing their finances, as it is often quite detailed. A financial advisor and a small business owner build a trusting relationship where they both strive for the business's financial success. This partnership can enable you to find valuable insights that foster growth and ensure the company survives.

They share broad expertise and can help you organize your taxes, design your investment approach, and manage the risks to your finances. Financial planners must understand both the business's plans and the market changes when crafting financial plans. With an advisor, firms can set goals that are not too far from reality. This covers examining the company's finances, managing its cash flow, and studying the circumstances of the economy in which the business works.

Being objective and unbiased is one of the main advantages of working with a financial expert. Normally, business owners are caught up in running the business, making it difficult to judge better financial strategies for the future. The advice of an outside advisor allows business owners to think clearly and calmly, making choices that are not based only on their feelings.

Furthermore, financial advisors help clients manage any financial risks they may face. They review possible financial risks and design ways to manage them by investing in different types of assets, buying insurance, or making use of other financial products. Early risk identification by advisors helps companies avoid experiences that could halt their development.

Financial advisors are also crucial because they help people manage their taxes. Any business owner may have difficulty with tax laws, but advisors can help a company meet the rules and find chances to reduce their taxes. This achieves better results for the company's finances and allows it to use its free funds to support growth.

You should be careful and attentive when making your choice of financial advisor. People who own businesses should assess advisors by looking at their skills, experience, and knowledge of their industry. To ensure the partnership runs smoothly, it helps to establish how you will communicate and what is expected from each person right away. Regular communication and discussions ensure the financial strategy remains lively and flexible.

The leading financial advisors include a personal flavor in their strategies. They realize that small businesses have specific needs and are determined to help their clients prosper. Usually, suppliers and buyers become partners who respect each other and agree on important goals.

Working with a financial advisor can significantly change the way a small business operates. It teaches them what they need to make their business successful in the future. With their support, business leaders take actions that link financial adjustments to the company's permanent goals and plans.

Utilizing Accounting Software

Using accounting software helps a small business become more effective and accurate in managing its finances. The impact of this development is seen clearly in businesses today since it allows them to handle their finances efficiently. Small business owners can now use accounting software to make accounting easier and improve their decision-making.

Hotels should begin by noticing the many benefits of using accounting software when deciding if they should adopt it. This technology allows many repeated financial tasks to be automatically performed. Among other things, it means preparation for billing, generating paychecks, and calculating taxes, which is usually quite time-consuming to do manually. Having automation decreases the chances of a mistake, so financial records follow industry best practices. For a company's financial statements to remain solid and reliable, added accuracy is vital for planning and forecasting.

With accounting software, leading business figures can monitor their finances at any given moment. This tool matters a lot to small businesses since managing cash flow is crucial for them. The fact that it manages accounts receivable and payable means entrepreneurs get insights to decide quickly on whether to collect debts or postpone making payments. Because of this, companies can easily manage and maintain the cash flow necessary for running and growing the business.

The software is useful because it makes it easy to create detailed reports of financial data. A business's financial condition can be seen clearly with reports such as profit and loss statements and balance sheets. With such knowledge, people can spot trends, review business strategies, and choose the best options. Entrepreneurs can also use custom reporting to look at particular aspects that matter for their businesses.

It is important to mention that the software helps businesses comply with necessary financial rules and standards. Proper record-keeping, made possible with accounting, reduces the risk of being penalized for not following rules. Since the software closely tracks every expense, it is easy to determine what costs can be deducted to reduce taxes. This factor helps small businesses, as they usually work with margins that can be greatly improved by receiving tax benefits.

Besides, using accounting software allows teams to connect and collaborate more easily. Because several users can access the financial data together, everyone can see the information and ensure it is handled efficiently. Because of this feature, remote team members and teams at different locations can all stay informed about the latest changes in the company's finances.

Put accounting software helps a business become more efficient and successful. Accounting software automates repetitive chores, delivers accurate and timely details, reports thoroughly, maintains compliance, and encourages joint work, allowing small business owners to deal with finance challenges smartly and without risk. Applying this technology is a means of modernizing your business, allowing it to grow and make profits over time.

CHAPTER 10

NETWORKING AND COLLABORATIONS

Understanding Networking Benefits

In pursuing small business ventures, networking turns out to be very important in shaping how successful a person can become. Networking is not only about collecting business cards or following people on social media; it gives you access to many important opportunities. By networking, entrepreneurs may find important information about the industry that they might not get otherwise. Such information can give a business an advantage, helping it keep track of market changes, adjust to changes in consumer preferences, and notice new trends.

Networking offers more than just finding out new information. It helps someone gain more recognition and strength in the industry. Both peers and potential clients can help entrepreneurs acquire a leader's influence and credibility. Because businesses are attracting more attention, they now gain access to potential partners and opportunities that could not have been available before.

You should have clear goals in mind when engaging in networking. If you want to succeed, set clear goals for your network, such as finding mentors, meeting potential clients, or working with others. The strategy ensures that networking activities are all part of the bigger plans, so they are more effective.

Being aware of the various types of networks allows us to use their advantages for our benefit. Being part of a professional network, having friends, and belonging to an alum community gives people various benefits. Being part of a professional network gives you industry-related knowledge and contacts. Support from personal connections can be encouraging, while alum networks usually help introduce you to people who might not be available to you otherwise.

To establish genuine and fruitful relationships, you must have a networking mindset. You must foster an interest in others and, in turn, be interested in what they have to say. You should first listen and offer your help before you expect anything from others. If entrepreneurs put effort into building honest ties with others, their network will help reach the business's objectives.

An effective elevator pitch should be a key part of your approach to networking. A good pitch explains what could make a partner or client choose your business. When you change your pitch depending on who will hear it, it leaves a positive mark on everyone you address. Injecting storytelling tactics makes the pitch more memorable and lively.

You should prepare and plan for networking events and meetups. Choosing the proper events for networking helps entrepreneurs use their hours efficiently. Asking open questions from a list and quickly introducing yourself can make any conversation more interesting. Group discussions and friendly body language while attending events can help you establish a good relationship with the other attendees.

Following up is crucial in the client-agency relationship. Sending a quick and personal message after an event allows you to nurture your connections. Connecting with people online through personal emails or messages on LinkedIn can help develop relationships for a longer period.

To put it simply, networking can help a small business grow and become successful. Networking plays an important role for entrepreneurs, helping them increase opportunities, learn from others, and form long-lasting partnerships.

Crafting an Elevator Pitch

An elevator pitch is a brief but powerful speech that makes people interested in a business idea or product. It aims to hold someone's attention and summarize the nature of a company in about 30 seconds to 2 minutes. The purpose is to make sure the audience remembers the main message about your company.

For a memorable elevator pitch, start by telling who you are and what you do briefly. You should begin with a sentence that makes your statement trustworthy and relevant. Establishing who you are, your work, and your business gives the other person a foundation to ask questions. Once that is covered, you need to demonstrate what the business provides that is unique or special (its USP). The USP ought to state what your business does better than others and highlight the benefits and solutions that appeal to potential customers or investors.

To see the best outcomes, the pitch must be adjusted based on who you are presenting to. Since interests differ among stakeholders, ensuring the content is suitable for all is necessary. While pitching to investors, emphasize the sound finances and possible growth opportunities within the company. Rather, focus on a potential client on how the product or service can handle their specific problems or satisfy their wishes.

Working on presenting the elevator pitch will help you look confident and involved. If you practice often, you can naturally respond to your audience and match the pitch accordingly. Recording your practice can help you learn from listening to your fellow musicians.

Telling a story during the pitch can increase its impact and interest. A fast example or a strong analogy may help the listener understand the value and importance of the business product. It attracts viewers and helps them relate to what is happening in the film.

In essence, to create an effective elevator pitch, you must be clear and brief and persuade your listener. The branding should make the business easy for people to grasp and remember. Having a good pitch increases the chances of positive discussions, more opportunities, and the formation of partnerships in the business world.

Navigating Networking Events

Networking events may feel exciting yet a bit intimidating to some people. Everyone is full of shining hopes coming together from various sources. You should be careful about the events you participate in to achieve the biggest rewards. A proper event suits your needs, giving you the chance to meet people who are important for your future. Exploring the subjects on the agenda and the backgrounds of the speakers can show if the event is worth attending.

You should be prepared before you visit any of these busy venues. Creating a brief introduction of yourself can help you move on to more meaningful chats. It should outline your unique qualities and highlights, hoping to prompt others to want to know more. Moreover, having some open-ended questions on hand can help you start talking about serious matters.

At the event, people shift their emphasis to interacting with others. Having a good conversation comes from being an active listener and truly interested in what others say. Discussions and breakout sessions allow individuals to share ideas with everyone and learn new things, as this approach draws in the wisdom of the group. Just by using eye contact and open body language, a person can appear open and interested.

The process continues even after the event ends. It's during the follow-up that one takes the first step toward a lasting connection. Sending individual follow-up communications on LinkedIn helps maintain the relationship started at the event. By mentioning what you discussed with someone, you can make your message both more impressive and more likely to be remembered.

Making connections should be viewed as setting up opportunities that will materialize in the future. Those attending these events might build professional relationships mentorships, and even make friends. Making the most of these events gives individuals a greater chance to expand their work network, understand the industry better, and discover new possibilities. Anyone wanting to advance in business or a profession should attend these events, as they offer a chance to highlight abilities, build relationships, and grow influence in the industry.

Building Online Presence

Nowadays, small businesses must establish an online presence to succeed. First, one must understand what the brand is all about, as this will guide all online actions. It involves building consistency in visuals, like a logo, preferred colors, and fonts, which deliver the brand personality to people using computers or mobile devices. The importance of keeping the voice and tone the same lies in helping people keep recognizing and trusting a brand.

A strong internet presence is built around an excellent website design. The website should be built to respond to people using mobile devices for easy access. The site must have easy-to-use links and eye-catching buttons so that guests follow the intended course. Beginning with SEO strategies, such as understanding keywords and adjusting the site pages, can strongly increase your chances of being found on search engines. Also, if the site responds quickly and is simple to use, it will hold onto users and keep them interested.

Social media allows businesses to reach and connect with their desired customers. Analyzing the audience is essential since different people use many platforms and offer distinct types of content. Ensuring each content strategy matches the audience of a particular platform gives you a better chance to reach them. Shareable things like visual and live content can bring followers together and build a community. A regular posting schedule made possible by a social media calendar keeps the audience interested.

Building an online presence is possible thanks to content marketing, which offers something valuable to the audience. Creating content means you must consider the brand's interests and what matters to its audience. Having exciting headlines and easy-to-understand content in your blog posts can encourage people to read your blog. Having videos and infographics on your pages improves content and aids in better search engine ranking. Using the right keywords and including links within your content is another way to raise your online presence and draw people.

Building relationships with both future and current customers can be done effectively through email marketing. If you want to develop an email list from nothing, you should use lead magnets and set up opt-in forms. Why? – When emails are carefully tailored to what different people want, they are more likely to engage and make a purchase. StreetLight Processing Inc. streamlines email communication and receives insights for improvement through analytics.

Looking after our online reputation is an activity that must be done all the time. It is important to answer messages and comments as quickly as possible and to respond positively to any negative opinions. Being visible in forums and groups connected to your industry allows your business to establish itself as a leader in the field. Those who share their experiences and insights with others can build a good online reputation for their company.

Overall, making your business visible online requires targeting branding, web design, SEO, social media, content marketing, and reputation management. Using these tools successfully, small companies can make their brands more visible in the digital world to their desired customers.

Establishing Partnerships

Making partnerships is generally necessary for entrepreneurship for any business to flourish and stay operational. Identifying partnerships that could be fruitful comes first. It requires you to understand the goals of your business and how an external organization could help you achieve them. There are various ways businesses can join forces, including holding events together, conducting joint brand campaigns, or making products together. Look for businesses whose skills are complementary to yours so you both gain from the partnership.

Once you know who the partners might be, you should approach them with a strategic plan. Establishing a strong proposal that demonstrates what your company and the partner hope to gain is very important. It is important to highlight your contributions as well as to explain how your business partnership benefits the other side in achieving their ambitions. Making common values and a long-range vision clear can help a company secure a partnership.

Negotiating and formalizing your partnership ensures that both parties can work from a stable position. Effective communication cannot be overlooked at this stage. Having an MOU or a similar agreement can assist in defining what each party will do in the partnership. At this stage, both individuals agree on their goals and methods, which helps avoid miscommunication.

Once the partnership is set up, it needs to be reviewed and cared for. Sharing thoughts and problems on a regular basis allows for quick problem-solving and maintains the smooth course of the collaboration. Showing appreciation for what has been achieved together can strengthen the bond between both parties. It is also necessary to check if the partnership is doing well, as agreed on, to confirm it continues to benefit both sides.

Yet, bringing two companies together can be challenging at times. Disagreements can arise when companies operate with distinct cultures, plans, or ways of doing business. Patience, flexibility, and willingness to change can help us overcome these problems. To build resilience in partnerships, accept feedback and listen to suggestions for making changes to the partnership approach or its structure.

In summary, to have a successful partnership, follow a plan from finding the right firm to managing your interactions together. Through active, open communication and having the same goals, businesses form valuable partnerships that help them succeed over the long run. Since forming partnerships is not easy and always requires work and commitment, the rewards are worth it—enhancing a small business in many ways.

CHAPTER 11

DIGITAL MARKETING

Building a Brand Identity

It is the sense of what a business stands for that gives it a distinct character and appeals to its target customers. This information is key for a small business to succeed, as it reveals what the brand stands for and why it is different. A brand identity is created by mixing appropriate visuals, such as what you say and how you say it, to share the main message of the business.

The first thing to do when building a brand identity is to set its core values and message. What the brand offers and guarantees to its customers mainly depends on these elements. A business's culture and key decisions are guided by its core values, and its brand message distills what the brand aims to achieve for its audience.

Images and designs are vital in expressing what a brand represents. For this reason, the logo, chosen colors, and lettering should be carefully chosen to show what the brand is like and to communicate well with the targeted audience. A good logo is the face of a brand, instantly known and capable of reminding people of the brand.

Paying attention to color psychology can help you understand how selecting a certain palette can influence people. Fonts selected for a brand can portray it as more professional or more welcoming to the audience.

The same brand voice and tone should be used in every message and platform to ensure the brand is recognizable everywhere. The brand voice shares the character of the business and its beliefs, while the tone may change depending on who you are talking to and the situation. When a business sticks to the same elements, customers recognize and trust the brand more easily.

Building a brand identity requires having well-planned guidelines for your brand. The guidelines explain how all communication and services should reflect the brand's image. It covers details on using the logo, choosing colors, selecting typefaces, setting the tone and voice, and allowing every action involving the brand to follow a uniform style.

Being online is essential for every brand to stay competitive today. A goal of this is to create a website that displays the company's plans and also expresses its identity through both style and content. Carrying out SEO practices is important for a brand, as it can improve its chances of being noticed and bringing in more organic visitors. Using social media lets a brand show its identity, so it is important to create and maintain content carefully for the audience.

To build a brand identity, you need to create an unforgettable and meaningful impact on your selected audience. To succeed, all segments of a brand's presence need to come together to make the brand story more convincing. In this manner, small businesses can stand out among competitors, keep their customers loyal, and prepare for continued growth over a long period.

Creating a Dynamic Website

Any small business aiming to succeed online should focus on creating a striking website. An effective website represents the business and lets potential customers learn about its values and products. First, the important features supporting both the usage and enjoyment of the website must be identified. A website that reacts smoothly to all devices is necessary to ensure both its accessibility and visual appeal on different screens. As a result, websites involving adaptive design are praised by users and have gained popularity with search engines.

A site's navigation should be simple and clear to make following the site effortless for anyone. If your website is well-structured and the menus are easy to use, people can access the information they need more easily and are less likely to leave without making a conversion. Having helpful call-to-action (CTA) buttons that guide users through specific steps, such as registering for newsletters or purchasing goods, is also necessary. The CTA needs to stand out and convey that it is worth clicking on.

Making use of essential SEO strategies is important to improve the presence of your site on the internet. You must research popular keywords and use them in your content to be visible to people online. On-page factors, such as writing good meta tags and alt text for images, help the site get noticed by search engines. Moreover, adding regular keyword-focused posts to a business blog ensures the website stays active and helps the company become a leading expert in its sector.

It is very important to prioritize user experience (UX). Fast loading of the site should be guaranteed, as users may become upset and navigate away from the site if it takes too long. By using Google Analytics, you can learn about the behavior of your users and see where you can make things better. Checking metrics such as bounce rate and session duration can help direct changes to the website.

Including links to social media websites on a website helps more people find the business and engage with the company. As a result, users come together, interact, and share what they find interesting.

It is necessary to regularly update and maintain the website to avoid problems and safeguard it. Checking the site and its content on a regular basis makes it useful and reliable. When SSL certificates are put in place, the site becomes more secure for users and more trusted by search engines.

Well-made websites help small business owners attract their customers, establish a successful brand, and move their business forward. The digital base aids in many marketing efforts and greatly contributes to building a successful business.

SEO Basics

Having a strong online presence is often made possible for small companies with SEO as a key feature of their digital marketing strategy. Increasing the visibility of a website on search engines allows businesses to get more free visitors and helps them succeed and stay alive online.

The main idea of SEO is to understand how search engines rank web pages through the use of algorithms. Such algorithms consider different aspects, including how relevant and high-quality the content is, how organized the web pages are, and whether keywords are included. Making use of these powerful elements can help small business owners get a better search ranking for their websites.

The first thing in SEO is to research keywords. This signals identifying the specific words or phrases that individuals use to find your product or service online. Both Google Keyword Planner and SEMrush can guide you in finding valuable keywords and checking their search numbers and level of competition. When the keywords are found, they should be included in website content, meta descriptions, and titles.

On-page SEO focuses on adjusting page content to improve its position and attract visitors from search engines. Adjust the titles, headlines, and content of your site to include the focused keywords and make sure it is not bland. Moreover, putting alt tags on your images and making your URLs neat can make your pages more visible to search engines.

The good technical performance of a website also helps with SEO. Having a site that can be accessed on mobile devices, loads quickly, and uses HTTPS increases its rank in search engines. To be noticed by search engines, it is best to review your website for technical issues and address them regularly.

Having links to your website from respected sites is also very important for SEO. They certify that a website is reliable and respected. Prospects for shareable content that others want to link to and becoming a guest blogger on well-known ones.

Small businesses working in certain locations benefit a lot from practicing local SEO. Optimizing a business for local search helps it appeal to customers living near the company. It requires listing the business on Google My Business, using the same business name, address, and phone number everywhere, and requesting feedback from customers.

Any SEO strategy must include monitoring and analysis. Google Analytics and Google Search Console both help you understand the number of people visiting your site, their actions, and your search results. By keeping an eye on the data, businesses figure out which business approaches need improvement.

Implementing these SEO methods in a company's plan can improve its visibility on the web, attract more buyers, and achieve greater sales and expansion of the business. Being informed about the newest SEO trends helps your business to remain competitive.

Leveraging Social Media

Nowadays, small businesses can use social media platforms to reach their customers, build recognition, and boost their sales. Learning these platforms' features allows a business to reach out in powerful and profitable ways.

The first thing to focus on is selecting the appropriate platforms for social media. Every platform targets different types of people and the things they are likely to do. While Instagram is mostly about images and is favored by young adults, LinkedIn is suitable for networking among adults working in professional fields. The first thing to do is to figure out where your target audience hangs out on social media.

After selecting the platforms, companies should work on creating content that people want to share. A good post is informative, meaningful, attractive to look at, and expresses the brand's personality. Posting great pictures, interesting videos, quizzes, or polls can lead to more interest from audiences. Share your customers' experiences and give people a glimpse into your work so they feel they can connect with you and believe in your brand.

Being regular on social media contributes to a strong presence there. Consider using a content calendar so you are aware of when to post and can schedule for notable events, holidays, or when you introduce new products. It's also designed to evenly mix promotions, learning content, and material posted by your community. Hootsuite or Buffer makes it possible to schedule posts and manage several accounts at the same time.

Maintaining contact with your followers is as important as uploading your videos. If you answer comments and messages right away, it will promote a stronger sense of community and let your customers know you care about their views. You could also organize QandA sessions or webinars to encourage more participation from your audience.

It is also important to analyze your data to figure out what kind of material your audience responds to best and how they connect with your company. Facebook Insights and Twitter Analytics collect information about your posts' outreach, their performance, and who your followers are. You should use this information to regularly improve your social media strategy so you are meeting your audience's likes and behaviors.

Along with using Facebook naturally, it is also a good idea for small businesses to pay for ads on social media to reach more people and target the groups they want. Both Facebook Ads and Instagram ads allow businesses to choose who will see the ads and react the most.

Overall, using social media in tandem with other marketing efforts makes them more effective. Likewise, link your website to your social media platforms, maintain the same visual style on all accounts, and add social media links to every email you send to your customers.

Basically, you should use social media strategies by studying the users on each platform, offering interesting content, remaining consistent in your interaction, and using analytical tools to guide your decisions. This allows small businesses to take advantage of social media to improve relationships with their customers and raise their profits.

Analyzing Marketing Metrics

Effective marketing analysis in small businesses forms a vital ability that can greatly contribute to the company's achievements. Metrics in marketing show business owners the way, giving them advice needed to make better business and marketing decisions.

You should first realize that marketing metrics play a key part in assessing whether a marketing campaign is effective or not. They let marketers track several ways the company performs in marketing, showing how customers act, how the campaigns perform, and how the company achieves a return on investment. When they review the metrics, company owners discover which things are working right, which need fine-tuning, and which offer new opportunities for improvement.

It is important to monitor the conversion rate because it shows how many people have taken a specific action, such as buying your products or signing up for newsletters. It is important to find out if the company's CTA works and how users feel using its website or app. When people convert frequently, it usually shows that the marketing strategy works, but when conversions are lower, changes are required in the messages, who is targeted, or the user interface.

Another important measurement is customer acquisition cost (CAC), which covers all the expenses needed to bring each new customer on board. It allows businesses to review how efficiently they are using their marketing funds to stay profitable. Having a lower CAC is good, as it results in stronger profit margins for the company.

CLV helps by determining the estimated revenue a business can earn from a customer over time. CLV to CAC is used by businesses to check that spending on customer acquisition is reasonable and should not be a burden. Where CLV is greater than CAC, it shows that the company is making money from its marketing strategy.

CTR and bounce rate are important factors for assessing the success of marketing activities. CTR demonstrates how many people took action after seeing an ad, while the bounce rate records the proportion of people who only visited one page on the site. A website with a good CTR and a low bounce rate usually indicates that its content is truly interesting and useful.

Secondly, likes, shares, and comments on social media can help one understand how visible a brand is and how much its audience interacts with it online. With these statistics, companies can adjust their content to meet the needs and interests of their target group.

Businesses should rely on analytics tools to correctly track all of these numbers. These solutions provide information that can assist in preparing reports, figuring out online trends, and adjusting marketing strategies. Frequent assessment of marketing metrics aids in developing a strategy, determining appropriate targets, and seeing how the business is progressing.

Collecting data is one part of marketing metrics, but a good marketing system analyzes them to promote growth and new ideas. With solid metric analysis, small business owners reach new chances to succeed, as their marketing is both well-performing and efficient.

CHAPTER 12

HANDLING CHALLENGES

Managing Cash Flow

In managing a small business, managing cash flow is extremely important. Every successful business relies on cash flow, which must be monitored and managed to prevent it from sinking. If you can manage your cash flow well, you might thrive, but if not, you could struggle to keep afloat.

The key to managing cash flow is understanding its basics. In addition to tracking inflows and outflows of money, one should also analyze cash flow statements to find out what patterns exist and what may lie ahead. Regularly reviewing cash flow statements allows businesses to find any trends that indicate if they might have too much or too little money so they can adjust their finances accordingly.

One must anticipate unexpected expenses to maintain good cash flow. Companies should maintain an emergency fund to cover new expenses that were not expected. This may be accomplished by saving money that can be used in case of emergency. Including a plan for unexpected expenses in the financial plan can give the business greater financial security during emergencies.

Managing both the receivables and payables better is also a vital strategy. Managing cash inflows effectively can help a business get paid on time. For example, you should issue invoices as soon as an order is filled and should ensure that unpaid bills are handled promptly. Alternatively, by negotiating with vendors and suppliers, companies can avoid incurring late fees and maintain their cash flow balance.

It is crucial to monitor and forecast your incoming and outgoing cash to keep the company from running out of money. To do this, you should use tools that predict future cash flow from the data you currently and previously recorded. The practice of having monthly cash flow review meetings allows owners of a business to know their finances and plan future actions or investments wisely. Since the issues are detected early, companies can effectively deal with them as soon as they appear.

Controlling cash flow requires managers to be adaptable. Any shifts in the market or business practices should lead to changes in managing cash flow. To maintain financial health for a long time, someone must be flexible. Any changes in a company's situation may require business owners to update their financial plans and strategies, ensuring their cash flow management is updated and still works well.

Basically, you need to plan, keep an eye on your cash flow on a regular basis, and always be flexible. If a business owner masters these aspects, their business will not just survive but may also grow and prosper. Cash flow management plays a key role in the success of a business.

Building Resilience

Entrepreneurship involves a lot of problems; therefore, resilience is necessary to help support business growth. To become resilient, the first thing to focus on is how to handle your cash flow. Knowing the financial situation allows the business to meet all its needs and be prepared for surprises. Preparing a good cash flow statement and reviewing it regularly, as well as setting up an emergency fund, should be part of an entrepreneur's routine. Using this strategy, entrepreneurs can handle shocks without interrupting their business processes.

At the same moment, avoiding fears of failure is vital. Dreading risks can keep someone from deciding or trying out new ideas, but identifying and handling them can help turn into a driving force. Writing in a journal allows us to see the reasons behind our fears, and transforming these thoughts using cognitive restructuring can boost our growth. It is important to view challenges positively and appreciate small successes, as they help one feel more confident and look at the world positively.

Planning is also very important for surviving in challenging situations. If entrepreneurs are well-prepared, they feel more assured and able to manage any tough situations that arise. They must participate in scenario planning and skills training to prepare for different situations in business. Also, being mentored helps to protect you and shows you the course you should follow. Gaining valuable advice and motivation can be achieved by making mentors and joining entrepreneurial groups.

The ability to cope with problems is greatly improved by studying your past mistakes. When mistakes are considered chances to hold training, employees and the company are always improving and growing. Analyzing after an outage and discussing it can reveal helpful information. By using brief iteration cycles, organizations are able to make changes quickly and respond well to competitors. Writing down what was learned during each task allows teams not to repeat their errors and to share what they have learned.

Being flexible is also necessary in any situation. Being flexible and open to change allows a company to shift its strategies when required and update its business approach according to feedback in the market. Organizations accomplish this by fostering a workplace where trying out new things is valued over sticking to the old way.

Long-term stability can be maintained by ensuring there is a balance between your work and personal life. Clearly, dividing your work and personal lives saves you from burnout and keeps you motivated. Making sure to exercise and practice mindfulness regularly supports both our thoughts and bodies. Managers should delegate tasks and plan breaks for leisure time so they are not exhausted.

Becoming more resilient involves regularly making changes and seeking the proper help and guidance. Emphasizing their finances, working through issues, learning as they go, and staying balanced help entrepreneurs succeed and advance in their personal and business lives.

Learning from Mistakes

Every entrepreneur needs to be able to learn from the errors they encounter. Many mistakes, if looked at differently, can help you learn and progress. When small business owners adopt this attitude, struggles can help them move closer to their future achievements.

The first phase requires making sure that the work environment sees mistakes as opportunities instead of failures. They need to ensure team members feel comfortable discussing and analyzing things they did wrong. Conducting autopsies on projects that failed can highlight the issues that affected them. The goal should be to find out why things went wrong so that the team can have a better plan for preventing these errors in the future. Using this approach helps create a learning atmosphere and allows everyone in the team to trust each other more.

Making change quickly after making mistakes is crucial for making progress. Since small businesses operate at high speed, being adaptable and adjusting strategies is very important. Owners of businesses should have fast feedback sessions to change the next version of their product or service. Thanks to this process, tiny changes can be implemented quickly, allowing people to learn from their mistakes.

Coming up with notes on what you learned from mistakes is vital as well. A record of the lessons learned from mistakes can be used in the future to inform and guide your choices. This way, no valuable knowledge is shed, and the team has an advantage from lessons it has learned earlier. Telling the team what I have learned helps everyone learn together and prepares the company for the future.

Being adaptable and flexible benefits a business owner hoping to learn from mistakes. Because the business world is always shifting, a firm strategy may result in a company standing still. Entrepreneurs ought to be flexible with their strategies and welcome changes as required. This generally requires adjusting how the company functions to fit market trends or adjusting products to keep up with customers' demands. If small business owners keep an open mind, they can address challenges on the way and still grow as a result.

Essentially, making mistakes and learning from them helps people develop a mindset that views problems as ways to improve. It involves making a business ready to handle trouble and actually improve due to it. If small business owners create a learning environment, repeat their actions regularly, record important lessons, and promote adjustment to change, they can benefit a lot from their mistakes. By doing this, the business becomes stronger, and entrepreneurs are given the skills and knowledge they need to handle changes firmly.

Maintaining Work-Life Balance

Ensuring a good balance between entrepreneurship and personal life matters most in today's world. Building and running a small business can often keep a business owner so engaged that personal health and relationships are put in the background. Still, it is achievable and very important for success and overall happiness in the long run.

Start by making it clear what you are and are not comfortable with. It helps entrepreneurs to decide on regular working hours and commit to following them as often as they can. By doing this, you can make sure your work life stays away from your time and vice versa. Setting up a specific workspace at home or work adds another barrier between your work and personal life.

Taking care of yourself is another important part of life. Staying active, engaging in mindfulness, and getting the rest you need is good for your health and boost your ability at work. Those who run businesses should routinely exercise, practice mindfulness sessions, or find time to relax. These activities benefit your health by increasing your energy and concentration.

Managing your work effectively becomes easier with the use of delegation. If entrepreneurs delegate certain tasks, they can spend more time on those that are most important to them. Sharing important tasks with team members reduces pressure on leaders and encourages employees to collaborate more.

Giving yourself time off is necessary as well. Owners of businesses should find time for frequent breaks and hobbies. The demands of being an entrepreneur are relieved by short trips, outings, and doing things you like. Participating in these events gives you a renewed sense of energy and new thoughts when you return to your job.

It is also important to adjust to new requirements in both your workplace and personal life. Adapting to new situations is very important. Those in business should learn to prioritize differently as requirements and situations change. Being adaptable helps ensure that both aspects of life are important, thus keeping motivation high and preventing constant fatigue.

The aim is to live in a way where career and personal time merge and are not in conflict. If the right balance is maintained, employees will be content, and the business itself will achieve more. Entrepreneurs can support their own and their business's growth by setting limits, focusing on themselves, assigning responsibilities, and making time for a break.

Dealing with Competition

Being competitive is a vital part of managing a small business. To do this, you must carefully consider the current market and foresee any coming changes. You should regularly check your competitors' actions and market trends to remain informed. You should monitor how your competitors act, price their products, create new products, and develop their marketing strategies. Assessing market information and other companies' activities can bring potential hazards and positive changes to your attention.

Being innovative is necessary to remain competitive in the market. Try to improve and distinguish your products regularly to make yourself different from others. You may organize innovation workshops or spend money on research and development to find new solutions. Strong innovation allows businesses to stand out and attract more customers.

It is also essential for a business to adapt to changes in the market. Consumer demands, the economy, and advancements in technology can bring changes to the business environment and the overall market. Adjusting to these situations with scenarios and flexible pricing can help your business handle new challenges. If you take action ahead of time, you can shift more easily and deal with any problems more efficiently.

Developing good customer relationships is important when it comes to competing. If customers remain loyal, a business will have an edge that others cannot match. Using customer feedback and providing personal service increases the chances that people will stick with the company. When you keep your customers satisfied, they will usually support your brand and help you gain new ones.

You can also use SWOT analysis to learn about your competitors to help shape how you position your company. Work on your strengths and attempt to close any gaps where others perform well. With this approach, you can spotlight what sets your business apart and share this information with your audience.

Promoting continuous betterment in your organization can support its continued growth and ability to compete. Letting employees accept change and appreciate feedback can ensure that products, services, and processes get better with time. This culture motivates staff members and also leaves a good impression on customers as well as in the market.

Overall, managing competition requires a combination of market analysis, driving innovation, adapting to changes, offering good customer service, and improving all the time. Combining these elements allows the organization to maintain a strong position compared to others in the market.

CHAPTER 13

SETTING LONG-TERM GOALS

Setting Long-Term Goals

When setting goals for a small business, protecting your future is much like building the foundation first. The initial vision for the company becomes a roadmap for each step the business takes in the future. When setting these goals, you should reflect, understand the market, and watch for upcoming trends.

Before creating long-term goals, one should look inside the company to identify what drives the business. Being aware of oneself is essential when planning goals. You should always think about your personal goals when making a business. Finally, I should consider how this business could influence the market and my situation. This information will guide the company and help define what it wants to accomplish in the long run.

When you identify what inspires your organization, ensure these motivations align with what is happening in the market. It is necessary to understand the market thoroughly. Here, one analyzes current developments, spots unmet needs that the business could address, and recognizes what problems may appear in the future.

Using this approach, entrepreneurs can identify long-term plans that are achievable and based on the market's needs and future openings.

A major part of planning for the long run is the capacity to face change and change your plan accordingly. There are regular shifts in business conditions due to changing consumer tastes, more advanced technology, and changes in the economy. Consequently, goals should be designed to deal with unexpected changes as they arise. Thanks to its flexibility, the business can adapt to new changes and grow instead of losing its place because of old and inflexible objectives.

Besides, long-term goals should be made into simple and achievable steps. Targeting these smaller tasks allows the business to achieve its big goals in stages. Celebrating achievements in the company allows employees to stay motivated, ensuring the main objective does not get forgotten while routine work is done.

It is best to use the SMART criteria to help develop long-term goals. Thanks to this approach, your goals are well-defined and can easily be put into action. Being precise reduces confusion while measuring makes it possible to observe results. Goals should be achievable to make them possible, stay relevant to the company's purpose, and be set on a timeline that matters.

Reviewing and revising your long-term goals should be done on a regular basis. When the business develops, and the environment changes, goals might have to be updated. By constantly establishing and checking new goals, the business can continue following its key objectives as the market changes.

Essentially, creating long-term goals means designing a plan that leads every area of the business. It involves finding a middle ground between dreaming big and seeing things clearly, being agile and disciplined, and being determined and patient. By setting worthwhile goals, entrepreneurs help their businesses grow and achieve their dreams.

Celebrating Achievements

As entrepreneurs build a small business, milestones and achievements show the way forward and help them succeed. Looking back at our accomplishments is significant, as it supports motivation and helps build a good team environment. Achieving any significant or minor step in a business gives everyone in the company a moment to reflect on their efforts and celebrate together.

Achievements are celebrated when we first appreciate the work of each person in the group. People should recognize how the team's actions together contribute to reaching their goal. Celebrating teams can involve easy recognition in meetings or bigger awards and social events organized for the team. They ensure employees feel like part of the group and aim to achieve even more because others notice and appreciate their efforts.

Additionally, marking achievements is a smart way to remind employees about the company's core beliefs and aims. Leaders can help the team focus on shared goals by connecting the company's celebrations with its main principles. If innovation is very important, praising achievements from a new launch or new idea inspires everyone to focus on innovation and be more creative.

We should also remember to recognize our achievements. Entrepreneurs and business owners ought to pause and recognize the achievements they have had in their careers. It might be possible to reward yourself by taking a day off or investing in a project close to your heart. Celebrating achievements at work ensures a good balance between your personal and professional life and prevents exhaustion.

Taking time to celebrate achievements lets you look back on the starting point and decide on any improvements that can be made. This allows us to keep improving and set better strategic plans. Many companies analyze their success factors, which they can use to guide future actions. On the other hand, noticing what can be done better helps a company update and enhance its plans for the upcoming achievement of goals.

Moreover, telling the world about achievements can increase a business's positive reputation and credibility. By posting successful stories through press releases, using social media, or sending newsletters, we celebrate the achievements of our team and, at the same time, help the brand look attractive to others and gain new clients and allies. It highlights the company as a leading brand that can fulfill its goals and succeed in what it does.

All in all, praising achievements is meant to maintain a positive energy that encourages further success. The idea is to acknowledge the hard work and the individuals who help accomplish the results.

Encouraging team members to focus on their successes and think about their achievements can inspire them to reach even bigger achievements.

Staying Connected to Purpose

Keeping a firm grasp on the original goals is crucial while starting a small business. It helps entrepreneurs make decisions when faced with various problems and difficulties. Essentially, the mission statement acts as a summary to define the main goals and values of the business. Focusing on the mission helps drive both entrepreneurs and their groups, as every move and plan is aimed at achieving the primary goals.

A mission statement should not just be written down and ignored. It should become part of daily activities, reminding the business of the reasons it exists and the customers it serves. Regularly discussing the mission within your team can help connect the team members and encourage them to feel their work matters. Through these discussions, members of a team are reminded of how their work helps achieve the organization's main goals and supports team spirit.

The mission message can also be displayed physically where team members work. Recalling these things in tough times re-energizes and inspires us. They act as a reminder to all employees about the company's key values and ambitions, encouraging everyone when they feel tired or unsure.

Continuously learning and finding inspiration from the world around you helps to preserve your sense of purpose. Taking part in industry events, reading materials by experienced entrepreneurs, and interacting with influential individuals may provide you with new ideas. They stimulate personal development and introduce new thoughts and directions for the company as the market changes rapidly.

Furthermore, celebrating what you achieve helps keep you enthusiastic and motivated. Highlighting individual and team achievements helps confirm the team's success in reaching the company's goals. They range from normal staff lunches to special ceremonies, as each one allows people to look back on their achievements and remember the common goals.

Remaining involved with your purpose is best achieved by taking the initiative. The process requires making long-term goals, reviewing them regularly, and adjusting them to continue with the mission as the environment changes. As a result, entrepreneurs can lead their businesses more smoothly and know where they are headed.

The nature of the journey through entrepreneurship involves achieving your goal just as much as it does sustain your founding purpose. When entrepreneurs embed their purpose in every area of business, they help the company grow and also maintain its true values.

Seeking Inspiration

The starting point for most small businesses is a bright idea, more than any other factor. Looking for inspiration involves making creativity thrive and caring for ideas, not only experiencing one brilliant moment. When beginning a small business, you must understand what leads to inspiration.

The beginning of the quest is to embrace curiosity. Curiosity allows us to discover new things and motivates us to explore and discover more about the world. Careers require us to pay attention to what is going on in the world around us and, at the same time, explore what we are passionate about. Mixing insights from outside and inside the organization often results in unique opportunities that can be changed into real business concepts.

Being observant is an important aspect of finding ideas. Entrepreneurs are advised to focus on the market and notice any missing or ineffective parts. A possible example is spotting that a town or city needs something missing or finding that people share the same problem with a product and it does not seem to be fixed. When we notice such findings, they can guide us in designing new answers to those needs.

Finding inspiration relies greatly on making connections. Discussing your business with other entrepreneurs, specialists, and people interested in your product lets you share new perspectives. Discussing ideas during conferences often inspires us to think differently and join forces to explore uncharted areas. By attending conferences, participating in workshops, and joining groups, individuals can gain new knowledge and connections.

Staying inspired involves reading and constantly gaining new knowledge. A wide range of knowledge and experiences can be found in books, articles, and case studies written by entrepreneurs who have gone through similar things. Being aware of what companies experience can help you learn new ways to address problems and find solutions. In addition, keeping up to date with the latest developments in technology and business methods and using educational resources often inspire new ideas in a company.

Being creative often comes naturally when we are permitted to experiment and take risks. Strong innovation can be achieved if failures are considered opportunities to learn rather than mistakes. Team members should be encouraged by entrepreneurs so they can try out new inventive solutions with minimal risk of failing.

Also, focusing on your inner life can greatly improve the way you discover new inspiration. When you take a break from your daily activities, you improve your ability to think clearly. Simply meditating, writing in a journal, or taking a walk outside can help you relax and think of new ideas.

So, being inspired happens as you open your mind, seek answers, and allow yourself to discover new things. Employing these principles helps small business owners upgrade their vision and respond to new trends and developments in the business world. As a result, entrepreneurs and the communities around them discover more chances and keep their energy and grit alive.

Continuous Learning

In the dynamic world of small business, the ability to adapt and evolve is paramount. This adaptability hinges on a commitment to continuous learning. Business owners must remain agile, constantly seeking new knowledge and skills to stay competitive and relevant in a rapidly changing market landscape.

Continuous learning for small business owners involves a proactive approach to acquiring knowledge and skills. This can be achieved through various avenues, such as attending workshops, enrolling in online courses, or participating in industry conferences. These activities not only provide valuable insights into current trends and practices but also offer opportunities to network with peers and industry leaders.

Moreover, reading is an essential component of continuous learning. Books, articles, and journals on entrepreneurship, industry-specific developments, and innovative business strategies can significantly enhance a business owner's knowledge base. By staying informed about the latest trends and technologies, entrepreneurs can make more informed decisions that positively impact their business operations and growth.

In addition to formal learning opportunities, practical experience is a crucial aspect of continuous learning. Engaging in hands-on projects, experimenting with new business models, and learning from both successes and failures can provide invaluable lessons. Entrepreneurs should embrace a mindset that views setbacks as learning opportunities rather than failures. This perspective encourages resilience and fosters a culture of innovation within the business.

Mentorship is another vital element of continuous learning. Establishing relationships with experienced mentors can provide guidance and advice that is tailored to specific challenges and opportunities. Mentors can offer insights based on their own experiences, helping business owners navigate complexities and avoid common pitfalls.

Furthermore, technology plays a significant role in facilitating continuous learning. Online platforms and digital tools offer access to a wealth of information and resources. Entrepreneurs can leverage these tools to enhance their skills, whether it's through webinars, podcasts, or virtual networking events. Utilizing technology effectively allows business owners to learn at their own pace and convenience, making it easier to integrate learning into their busy schedules.

Continuous learning also involves fostering a culture of learning within the organization. Encouraging employees to pursue professional development not only enhances their skills but also contributes to the overall success of the business. Providing access to training programs and learning resources can empower employees and increase their engagement and productivity.

Incorporating continuous learning into the business strategy ensures that the company remains innovative and competitive. It helps identify new market opportunities, adapt to changes, and meet customer needs more effectively. As the business landscape evolves, those who prioritize continuous learning will be better equipped to lead their organizations to sustained success.

Ultimately, continuous learning is not just a strategy but a mindset. It requires a commitment to personal and professional growth, a willingness to embrace change, and an openness to new ideas and perspectives. By embedding continuous learning into the core of their business practices, entrepreneurs can drive innovation, enhance their leadership capabilities, and create a resilient and adaptable business poised for long-term growth.

CHAPTER 14

ENSURING COMPLIANCE

Understanding Regulations

Everyone starting a small business needs to understand the rules and regulations carefully. Through enforcing regulations, businesses are guided to act fairly, protect customers, and maintain an orderly market. Understanding these laws may seem complicated, especially for new entrepreneurs. A good understanding of the rules is important to run your business within the law and do well.

The first thing to do is find out which rules and standards apply to your business and its area. Research should be done on the rules and laws related to your field since they may change a lot depending on that area. So, food service companies have to follow health and safety rules, while financial service providers must meet strict laws about data protection. It's important to know these requirements more than to prevent fines; you want your business to reflect the best ways of doing things that earn your customers' trust and support.

Being licensed and certified is necessary for following regulations. If your business is in certain fields, you will need to get certain licenses or certifications to work legally. Depending on your industry, your business may require just a basic business license or specialized certifications that confirm you meet set industry standards. Often, getting these licenses involves completing a detailed form, providing documents, and paying the necessary fees. You should be careful when following the process so that your business is not delayed or rejected.

It is also necessary to make a compliance plan as part of dealing with regulations. It gives your business a framework for consistently accomplishing its operations within legal limits. A good compliance plan usually has a list of regulatory rules, a plan for routine audits, and a format for reviewing the plan itself. Reviewing and auditing records often helps identify places where compliance is not met and take immediate solutions.

Equally, it is necessary to make sure staff are trained on compliance issues. Ensuring your staff is informed about regulations in your business helps you avoid breakage and consequences. Workshops and training events help you explain these requirements to the team. Also, preparing a compliance manual explaining standard procedures and guidelines is useful for everyone by ensuring everyone is following the same protocols.

Changes in laws happen over time, so staying informed is very important. To keep up with new developments, sign up for newsletters, get involved with professional groups, and use the advice of legal pros. Making connections with other professionals in your area helps you learn how they respond to new rules and find useful ways to cope.

Small business owners who are aware of and follow the rules can successfully build their businesses and stay away from legal problems. Taking this approach helps the business and stakeholders and also improves its reputation with the public. Hence, knowing rules is more than just being compliant; it helps a business to earn respect and develop.

Developing a Compliance Plan

Understanding and complying with the rules is an important part of beginning any small business. A thorough compliance plan is necessary for a business to obey rules, function well, and be honest. The process starts with getting familiar with the laws that govern your industry and area. Those who want to start a business must know about the specific type of regulations they must comply with.

Constructing a compliance plan is about designing a methodical strategy to meet all legal needs. The basis of the plan is building detailed compliance lists that point the way for the business to follow legal requirements. With these guidelines, the company can ensure that all parts of its work, both in operations and with employees, meet the country's requirements. Through regular audits, the plan can quickly find and address any issues in compliance before they turn severe.

Teaching your team about compliance is essential. People working in those roles should know the regulations that apply to them. It can happen by making employees aware of their responsibilities and the possibilities if these aren't followed using workshops and classes. Having a complete compliance manual gives employees instructions and processes to use in diverse situations.

Keeping up with changes in regulations helps ensure companies remain compliant in future periods. Since regulations are always changing, keeping up with them matters a lot for any business. siguir newsletters de la industria y consultar con abogados puede ayudar a los negocios a estar al tanto de nuevas developmentes. Being involved with professional contacts in the industry shows how businesses overcome new regulations.

Following a compliance plan means constantly focusing on ethical business activities. Stakeholders must identify any threat in advance and quickly respond to changes in regulations. Putting compliance into the work environment allows entrepreneurs to create a reliable and responsible company that gains customers' and partners' respect.

In addition, a sound compliance plan can give a company an advantage in the market. Businesses that routinely follow regulations are usually seen as credible by stakeholders and can compete differently in their industry. As a result, customers might be more loyal, and businesses could team up with others who care about compliance and morals.

A compliance plan, in reality, helps a small business achieve and maintain its success over time. It protects the business legally, increases how well it operates, and forms a base of trust and reliability. Starting a business as an entrepreneur, it's important to integrate compliance to achieve both legality and a well-respected business operation.

Training Staff

Small businesses rely heavily on good staff training to help them reach success. What matters most in training is encouraging a setting where people always learn, respond to changes, and support the company's strategic goals. Good training programs are carefully designed to boost everyone's abilities so that all team members can help the company achieve its objectives.

The first part of training is to assess the needs thoroughly. You can discover the team's skill and knowledge gaps through appraisals and by listening to feedback from staff. Learning about these gaps helps businesses offer useful training, which increases the value of their human resources. Ensuring that training targets match the company's business goals means those skills will help the company stay ahead in the market.

Next, a curriculum needs to be made that is both fun and useful. The best approach is to combine classroom learning with practical activities that help staff immediately use their new skills. Different training methods, such as workshops, seminars, online classes, and mentoring, appeal to a range of learners and help the training program work better. Besides, the use of online platforms for learning helps small business employees adjust their schedules whenever they need to.

Training centers greatly on the impact of leaders. Leaders should live by the commitment to learning, helping their teams learn and grow by leading by example. Being truly involved in the progress of their team can inspire leaders and team members to learn and advance steadily. Including constant feedback and coaching in training gives staff constructive ideas and leads them to work toward better outcomes.

Having students learn together as a team matters a lot. Having staff collaborate in teams and learn from others can improve the learning process for everyone. When teams join forces in this way, it draws the organization together and helps everyone feel like they're part of something bigger.

The success of a training program depends on giving evaluation and feedback. Determining how to test the results of training programs is important. Among these, performance, what employees can do, and how happy they are belong to the important metrics. Looking at these metrics often helps business owners change their training approaches to keep up with the needs of their teams.

All in all, small business training requires strong planning, proper execution, and effective evaluation. Developing people supports the most important resource any company has—its workforce. A good training plan not only increases the skills at work but also encourages the business to move ahead with innovative approaches and reach its goals. With a focus on training, small businesses can create a team that can deal with whatever challenges come their way in the current market.

Monitoring Changes

Because small business operations keep changing, they need to notice and adapt to any changes. Because markets, what shoppers want, and technology update quickly, companies have to watch for changes that could influence their growth constantly. They must find good ways to track these shifts so the business can react quickly to both new challenges and opportunities.

Taking care of these measures first by assembling a well-rounded framework that includes different parts of the business environment. To do this, businesses frequently create systems to gather and analyze information on market trends, what consumers do, and the actions of competitors. Reviewing market analysis and getting customer feedback gives useful ideas about the way preferences are shifting in the market. When informed, a business can predict upcoming trends and make the necessary adjustments to keep its advantage over others.

New technologies help shape the business world, so following what's new is very important. Setting up the right technology to follow changes should be a priority for businesses. The company does this by using data analytics platforms to view real-time information about sales, customer feedback, and day-to-day business issues. With these technologies, businesses can adjust their operations quickly to adapt to recent changes.

To manage change, organizations must prize flexibility and ongoing knowledge gained in their culture. If employees believe that change is a chance for growth, the business will be better prepared for any external changes. Organizing frequent sessions and workshops on new trends and technologies can provide employees with the abilities they need to meet changes.

Being involved in networking and teamwork is key to keeping a watch on changes. Getting involved with peers, going to conferences, and joining professional groups provide important information about where the industry is moving. By interacting with outsiders, business leaders may learn about things they hadn't considered within their organization and be ready to act on changes early.

In addition, companies should build a way to collect and analyze tips and comments from customers, staff, and stakeholders. This helps us see how others view changes and what effect they have on various parts of the business. When they listen to what these voices say, businesses have a chance to better fit their plans to what others in the community and market need and expect.

Plans should be able to change flexibly according to the needs of the company. It means you should be prepared to adjust or change your strategies when there's new or unexpected news in the market.

Having various plans in place can help a company overcome different risks and benefit from various chances.

Overall, it is important to monitor shifts when running and building a small business. With strong monitoring, new technologies, a flexible work culture, ongoing learning, and open relationships with stakeholders, businesses manage the challenges brought about by a changing market environment well. By being proactive, companies can prevent risks, spot new chances, and grow steadily into the future.

Auditing and Reviews

The beginning of any small business should include putting a proper system for auditing and reviews in place. Thanks to these processes, companies can function smoothly, obey regulations, and reach their strategic targets. Auditing, in short, is the methodical checking of financial records, systems, and processes to confirm everything is correct and up to code. Contrastingly, reviews regularly measure business performance by checking how things are done and if strategies are being followed.

A small business needs to decide both the scope and the regularity of its audits when starting the auditing process. Ongoing audits show where there are issues and allow them to be handled before they get worse. Any organization can do these audits internally or outsource them to professional auditors, each giving the business new perspectives and advantages. Internal auditing is effective for keeping an eye on operations and improving internal oversight. External auditing provides a fresh opinion and helps gain stronger stakeholder trust.

An auditor uses several important steps in the process. The first step is to plan what you want to achieve and how wide the project should be. This part of the audit process serves to decide which path you will take. At this point, data is gathered by reviewing statements, questioning employees, and observing in the workplace. Next, auditors analyze the information to compare it with the set requirements and benchmarks for that industry. An audit ends by producing a report that identifies points of concern and provides appropriate recommendations, both of which guide decision- and action-making for the future.

Even though reviews are closely connected to audits, they are not applied in the same way. Because they are less structured and more frequent, these meetings allow management to evaluate both the strategies and operations of the business. While financial, operational, and strategic, these reviews look at different businesses. Financial reviews check the company's financial position by studying factors including profitability, liquidity, and solvency. A focus of operational reviews is to discover if business processes are efficient and if all resources are properly used. On the other hand, reviews of strategies look at how the company's activities fit with its long-term plans to confirm it is moving forward toward its vision.

Having a clear auditing and review system in place for a small business brings many benefits. It increases openness and reliability, earns trust from investors and customers, and helps the company succeed by staying ahead of the competition. Additionally, when these processes show where they can be improved, businesses can work on optimizing how they operate, lower costs, and make more profit.

Small businesses need to support an ongoing effort to do things better in developing an effective auditing and review system. This covers asking for feedback, responding well to changes, and making sure that audits and reviews help you develop rather than simply following the rules. As a result, businesses maintain healthy current activities and set themselves up for future achievements. In essence, a business should be flexible, take advantage of fresh opportunities, and always perform at the highest levels while staying very ethical.

CHAPTER 15

PLANNING FOR THE FUTURE

Developing a Strategic Vision

A business strategy plays a crucial role in helping a new small business succeed. Rather than being a simple statement, this vision gives direction to the business from its beginnings through to its development. Making a strategic vision calls for careful self-reflection and knowing exactly what your motivations and dreams are. It clearly demonstrates what the business hopes to do and the role it wants to play in its area and industry.

The process starts with thinking deeply about the main reasons you want to start a business. To do this, we question ourselves by asking simple questions like "What motivates me?" and "Why am I starting this venture?" Reflection on these life experiences helps determine your goals and dreams, which create the core of the strategic vision. A clear vision matches up with personal motivators, keeping the business consistent with the founder's goals and core values.

As soon as you understand what motivates you, the process moves on to creating a meaningful vision statement. This phrase needs to be direct, brief, and inspiring to lead the business community. It outlines what the business wants to achieve over the long term and guides everyone. A vision statement isn't only a statement—it also guides business activities towards completing goals.

A viable vision can only be achieved when a clear mission statement supports it. A vision statement describes the company's long-term goals, while the mission statement gives directions for how to reach those ambitions. The mission statement outlines the business' aims, important values, and how it will care for its customers. An excellent mission statement gives guidance to employees on what to do every day and how to decide.

A clear link between vision and mission is very necessary. They need to collaborate so that the company's messaging and strategy do not change. If employees, investors, and customers all recognize the company's goals and the ways to hit them, communicating with them will become easier.

Because businesses compete fiercely in the small business sector, their strategy needs to adapt as needed. It must change along with changes in the market, what customers think, and the company's progress. Looking over the vision and mission statements from time to time helps them stay inspiring and up to date. Being flexible helps managers keep their team motivated and leads the business through all its developmental stages.

Moreover, a clear strategy differentiates your organization from others. It makes the business noticeable in the market by pointing out what is special about it. Telling people this vision frequently allows businesses to establish a well-known brand and strong relationships with both their customers and employees.

Essentially, a strategic vision describes in clear detail how the business wants to be developed moving forward. You need to use introspection, be clear in your mind, and think strategically. A well-defined vision and mission help entrepreneurs handle the difficulties of business development with direction and confidence.

Establishing Succession Plans

When running a small business, make sure you have a sturdy succession plan set up to protect its future and preservation. The plan is not only used in case of crises but also serves as a way to help achieve the company's future goals. This process concerns choosing and training people who will step in when previous ones retire or exit. By succession planning, the company ensures it has skilled workers who are ready to take over as managers soon become available.

Before anything else, you must assess the present management and leadership system. You should find out who holds important roles, examine what they do, and see what qualities their replacements will need. Thanks to this analysis, we can identify opportunities and needs for training and growth within the organization.

Succession planning depends on the ability to spot leaders in the organization. One has to fully grasp the types of capability, skills, and qualities that match what the business wants to achieve. Internal transitions are usually preferred because the candidates know well how the company operates and thinks. Still, organizations might bring in external candidates because they need new ways of thinking or different abilities.

Succession planning uses training and development programs to prepare future leaders for their tasks. Each program needs to focus on helping the business and the individual, working on their leadership, thinking skills, and ability to make choices. Being mentored by senior executives provides important insights and support to those just beginning their careers.

Besides preparation and coaching, it's necessary to inform everyone involved about the succession process and their roles. By offering transparency, organizations encourage staff and stakeholders to trust and adapt without issues.

Updating and evaluating the succession plan frequently will help it keep up with shifts in the company's environment, changes in its organization, and employees' goals. The plan stays current and useful because it responds to new challenges and opportunities as soon as they arise.

Also, the succession process should fit in with the business's main strategic plans. It needs to focus on the long-term vision and mission so that leaders who follow will have what they need to achieve the organization's goals. Because of this connection, the company is able to thrive even as the market evolves.

In short, it is important to develop a succession plan as part of an effective business strategy. It maintains the business's progress by helping new leaders take over smoothly, building a strong learning environment, and matching leadership abilities to business goals. With succession planning, a small business guarantees its future and ensures it stays solid.

Building Brand Legacy

For entrepreneurs, creating a renowned brand reputation is something more than just accumulating money or increasing their share of the market. It's about weaving a brand into the everyday life of the community so it is relevant for years to come. A good first step in building a lasting legacy is to get a strong understanding of the brand's main values. These values direct every choice and action inside the company. Like all good brands, they help create consistency and genuine values, both of which are important in an era when people are more informed.

Building a lasting impression starts by giving a brand an identity that is both recognized and valuable. It's not simply a case of images or slogans; a brand's identity includes every customer interaction. All the moments consumers have with a brand—including products, services, and support staff—affect their opinion of the brand. The meaning people attach to a brand is what gives it a unique place with them.

Also, telling stories is crucial for establishing a lasting image for a brand. Stories help us communicate values and reach people by touching their emotions. When a brand story resonates, it introduces its background and key goals while encouraging customers to be a part of what's coming next. Emotional links with the brand bring about loyalty and support, which are key to any strong brand legacy.

Along with telling stories, consistent messaging matters a lot. Trust is formed when you are consistent, and it is essential for any strong relationship to last. No matter the method—marketing, chatting on social media, or customer service—the brand's way of speaking should always be the same. By keeping things consistent, the brand lets customers trust it and feel more attached to it.

Being innovative is very important in building a lasting brand legacy. If a brand doesn't evolve, it can become unimportant to consumers. All of these efforts mean the brand stays current and appealing to its customers day after day. The company's values should not be risked when pursuing innovation. Rather, this should happen smoothly alongside them so that all new ideas stay true to the brand.

Involving the community is very important for building a lasting brand legacy. A brand that participates in community activities, supports local groups, and remains connected with its audience is appreciated and remembered by its audience. The company is focusing on making the community a better place to be, which will raise its reputation and keep it connected with its people.

Being flexible is important for a brand to surpass market and customer changes. Companies develop this resilience because of strong leadership, a firm vision, and the ability to change with time. Being aware of new trends and what customers think allows a brand to change its approach and keep building its history.

Really, making a successful brand legacy calls for strong commitment and a sincere concern for what the brand represents and its community. It is all about making something that lasts and continues to do well even as the business world changes. A successful brand legacy touches everyone, lasts in their memory, and encourages them.

Ensuring Financial Stability

Financial stability is very important for small businesses to achieve lasting success and strength. The first step in creating a strong financial foundation is to know how your business finances work. That means maintaining careful records and using valid bookkeeping methods. With digital tools, managers can stay more accurate and efficient with money, which makes it easier to check financial records and meet tax requirements.

Creating a complete financial plan is very important for maintaining financial security. The plan should explain all its sections, such as the allocation of startup funds and the development of cash flow forecasts. As a result, business owners can be ready for upcoming financial challenges. Applying scenario analysis helps companies model diverse financial results, which makes it easier for them to adapt to changes in the market.

A major factor is to make sure your financial goals are attainable. Once there is a clear purpose for the business and clear steps to get there, money decisions become focused and guided by the business's vision. Applying the SMART method—having your goals be Specific, Measurable, Achievable, Relevant, and Time-bound—helps make setting financial goals easier. Furthermore, setting up key performance indicators (KPIs) supports tracking results and making important changes when needed.

Diversifying revenue generation helps reduce financial risks. When businesses have several sources of income, they can handle market changes. Companies engage in diversification by growing their products, entering other industries, or teaming up with others to create new opportunities.

Stability can be improved by creating a financial reserve. Building a reserve fund with part of their profit allows businesses to deal with unexpected problems or market drops. Having this reserve helps the government manage economic difficulties while continuing to obey quality and efficiency standards.

Getting regular reviews of your finances is necessary to keep your money in good shape. Regular reviews help businesses evaluate finances in light of their goals and act smartly using recently finished information. The financial statements, cash flow statements, and financial ratios should be looked at and analyzed as part of these reviews to judge the business's operating performance.

Additionally, software programs that manage accounting reduce the time needed to review finances, making real-time information available for making better choices. These programs make it easy for business owners to follow financial statistics and create reports that point out important trends and places for improvement.

Having financial security depends mostly on taking a proactive approach to managing your finances. Paying attention to the industry, responding well to changes, and keeping financial strategies updated allows companies to grow sustainably. If a business is handled responsibly, it can do well and flourish in today's changing economy.

Preparing for Long-Term Success

Founding a lasting business requires solid planning at the beginning. Everything starts when a strategy is made that matches the key values and long-term purpose of the business. Thanks to this vision, the business is directed toward its goals even as factors in the marketplace change. In leadership workshops, teams look at different possible future scenarios so the business can get ready for both challenges and opportunities ahead.

Having a strong succession plan is very important for lasting success. Offering mentorship and tracking talented employees guarantees that when the current leaders are gone, the business will still succeed. When leaders develop this way, the company's achievements endure, and stakeholders feel sure the business will endure as well.

Creating a reliable brand image and a great reputation is essential for continuing success. A unified message from the company and acts of corporate social responsibility help the company keep a good reputation with its customers and neighbors. Adopting one brand identity repeatedly encourages trust and loyalty, which are critical to a business's success over time.

Strong finances are important for facing economic ups and downs and unusual issues. Taking these measures gives businesses something to fall back on in bad economic times. The company keeps its financial situation stable by regularly reviewing and auditing with help from our experts.

Along with financial preparation, you need to focus on new ideas and keep up with what's current in the industry. Companies improving with each new technology and responding to new customer needs are in a stronger position to take advantage of new opportunities. If employees are allowed to test and learn in the workplace, it helps the organization become competent and relevant in their field.

Besides, nurturing a culture that encourages continual growth matters a lot. Getting employees to participate in change efforts and using feedback to make these efforts ongoing helps the business improve and optimize what it does. Acknowledging achievements helps everyone feel good and reminds us all to aim for excellence.

For a company to stay successful over time, it must comply with industry rules and maintain high quality. Standardizing how work is done and offering training to staff help quality stay consistent as the business expands. Automation can contribute to better operational results and higher quality.

Good relations with customers, partners, and the community are essential for a company to succeed in the long run. Attention to customer satisfaction and the use of strong partnerships will help businesses increase their impact and audience. Taking part in community projects and keeping conversation lines open with stakeholders supports the business's reputation in the market.

In short, being ready for long-term success means combining strategic planning, improving leadership, ensuring financial health, sharing innovations, constantly improving things, checking quality, and building relationships. Focusing on these areas helps a small business grow and prevail in a tough business setting.

We'd Love Your Feedback!

Title:

Starting A Small Business
We'd Love Your Feedback!

Thank you for reading **Starting A Small Business**. We hope you found it insightful and valuable.

If you enjoyed the book, we would be incredibly grateful if you could take a moment to leave a review on Amazon. Your feedback not only helps other readers discover the book — it also supports our work and makes a big difference.

Simply scan the QR code below or visit the link to share your thoughts.

- Or visit: https://a.co/d/6FEi5zG
- Or visit our website: https://synastbooks.com

With heartfelt thanks,

CAMERON BANKS

www.ingramcontent.com/pod-product-compliance
Lightning Source LLC
Chambersburg PA
CBHW070810220326
41520CB00055B/6849